exotic
Gardening

exotic
Gardening
IAN COOKE

THE CROWOOD PRESS

First published in 2010 by
The Crowood Press Ltd
Ramsbury, Marlborough
Wiltshire SN8 2HR

www.crowood.com

British Library Cataloguing-in-Publication Data
A catalogue record for this book is available from the British Library.

ISBN 978 1 84797 213 2

Acknowledgements
Gardeners are generous creatures, and in the writing of this book so many have shared with me their knowledge and gardens, and have given me permission to use their photographs where I had none. I particularly thank Will Giles for inspiration, Tim Miles for a fascinating but wet day at the Cotswold Wildlife Park and Paul Spracklin for information and pictures on arid plantings. Thanks to Tim and Tracey in Retford and Tony Hoffman for letting me photograph their private gardens.

My appreciation for photos goes to Tom Cooke, Fergus Garret, Maureen Gilmer, Jon Kelf and Melissa Scott. Special gratitude to Mike Bates for the historic picture of Battersea Park sub-tropicals. I also applaud Mike Coleman and Tony Hallam for their patience, demonstrating propagation and planting whilst I wielded a camera.

And finally, thanks to my partner Philip, who has endured my single-minded concentration on this project, corrected my grammar, made valuable suggestions and poured recuperative wine when needed!

Picture Credits
All pictures by Ian Cooke except p. 13 Mike Bates, p. 17 Fergus Garrett, p. 18 Jon Kelf, p. 23 (lower), p. 14, p. 83, p. 103 and pp. 106–8 Melissa Scott, p. 74 and p. 147 Tom Cooke, pp. 110–11 Paul Spracklin, and p. 114 Maureen Gilmer

All pictures were taken in UK exotic gardens with the exceptions of pp. 37, 77 (left), 107 (right), 114, 121 and 163.

Front cover photograph: Jon Kelf

Typeset by Jean Cussons Typesetting, Diss, Norfolk

Printed and bound in Malaysia by Times Offset (M) Sdn Bhd

CONTENTS

PREFACE

Close your eyes and dream ... well maybe just read on and imagine for today! Huge floppy banana leaves, rustling palm fronds, towering bamboos, big blowsy blooms and swags of colourful creepers. All the razzle-dazzle of a tropical landscape!

I wonder what exotic destination you have conjured up in your mind? I guess it's some overseas holiday location, maybe the Canary Isles, Hawaii, California, Florida or even the Brazilian rainforest. But in my mind, I'm just down the road in one of a number of wonderful jungle-like gardens that enthusiasts have created in the inhospitable climate of the United Kingdom.

Surprising as it may seem, the temperate climate of the British Isles is ideal for growing a vast range of plants, including many that we wouldn't expect to see within our small chilly island. Plants from South America, China, Australia, New Zealand and even South Africa are all to be found side by side in nurseries and gardens. In recent years, a number of devotees have dabbled with the seemingly impossible and have created successful exotic jungle gardens, full of luxuriant growth and dazzling flowers, in the most improbable of locations.

Over the years I have dabbled with exotics whenever the opportunity has allowed. I have collected exotic plants, used them in displays I have created, and for a brief while I ran my own nursery, Brockings Exotics. For some years I held the National Collection of Canna, which grew to an unwieldy assortment of some 500 different species and cultivars

OPPOSITE PAGE: **A lush mixture featuring *Musa sikimensis*, New Zealand flax, bamboos and other foliage in the walled garden at Highfields House at the University of Nottingham.**

from all over the world. Sadly it is no more, having been devastated by virus which swept through the collection.

Way back in the 1980s whilst working at Reading University, I designed an exhibit for the local flower show called 'Clearing in the Jungle'. It was a fanciful creation using colourful plants set around a shallow pool, complete with floating water hyacinth and a ruined temple built from vast lumps of masonry from the local reclamation yard. Our display of cannas, bananas, palms and ferns looked fabulous, set amongst the tables of prize-winning cakes and the cages of award-winning fur and feather. To our delight, it won best in show, and I become 'hooked' on this fanciful and theatrical style of gardening.

For the last fourteen years, whilst at the University of Nottingham, I have again indulged my interests and created an exotic landscape within the high brick walls of the old garden at Highfields House. Against a background of bamboos and other hardy exotics, each summer we added a seasonal display of sizzling cannas and colourful summer transients. The garden is now mature with soaring bamboo canes, thin spires of eucalyptus and well-established bananas with groves of chunky stems. What began as a whim is now a much-loved feature and quiet oasis, appreciated by the thousands of staff, students and visitors that use the University campus. The garden has been featured on television, and many of the pictures for this book were taken there.

We may not have tropical weather in the UK, but exotic gardens are HOT! Although this book is written from the perspective of the UK, where I live, it is intended for use by gardeners in all temperate regions of the world. An exotic garden is like a holiday that doesn't end. Enjoy it all summer long!

EXOTICISM

So what is an exotic? Most people would think that exotic plants mean unusual tropical plants, big lush specimens with huge leaves and sumptuous flowers, growing in an Amazonian jungle or coddled in a hot-house. In terms of this book, this is partly true, and many of the plants we will use will have fabulous foliage and flamboyant flowers. This is undoubtedly the exotic effect, but such plants don't have to be tender or tropical in origin. There are many exotic-looking plants that are fully hardy, tough and easy to grow, and you will discover more about them in the next chapter.

If we want to be botanically correct, an exotic plant is any plant that is not native to the country where we live. In the United Kingdom, there is actually a very small range of plants that are true natives, and in garden terms many of them are uninspiring. The vast majority of wonderful plants with which we fill our gardens come from other countries or have been produced by plant breeders over the centuries. It is these that are correctly referred to as exotics. How-ever for the purpose of this book we are going to stay with the generally understood meaning of the word: 'a plant that gives an exotic effect'. In fact this is not totally wrong; checking the dictionary, we find that exoticism is 'the charm of the unfamiliar', and this gives us a clear direction to the style we are exploring.

OPPOSITE PAGE: **The spiky foliage of _Cordyline australis_ 'Variegata' and waving leaves of bananas line this dark and mysterious entrance to the exotic garden at East Ruston Old Vicarage near Norwich.**

The Exotic Look

Many of the plants that we will be looking at qualify as exotics because of their foliage. Any plant that has large leaves will be effective at grabbing our attention. It will stand out as being exuberant and immediately says 'Hey look at me, I'm bigger than all the rest!' Plants such as palms, bananas, _Gunnera_, _Catalpa_ and _Tetrapanax_ all have leaves far larger than the average garden plant. Most exotic gardens will include a proportion of plants with variegated or coloured leaves. Coloured foliage from plants such as the multicoloured _Canna_ 'Durban' or the rainbow-hued coleus are certain showstoppers!

Spiky plants or 'spikies' as they are often dubbed, are also very valuable additions to any planting scheme and particularly so in the exotic garden. By their very nature, most will have narrow linear leaves, and many will have a strong architectural outline. Spikies add punch to a planting scheme and contrast well with broader paddle-like leaves. Ornamental grasses, New Zealand flax and _Yuccas_ are familiar examples of spiky plants. When we start to look at desert plants later on, we will explore the many other possibilities amongst spiky succulents such as _Agaves_ and _Aloes_. As well as spikies, there are many other plants with bold outlines that we can use, such as the palms. Their shape is distinct and unlike almost anything else in the plant world. Of course many palms come from tropical areas, and so whenever we see a palm, whether hardy or tender, we tend to think of exotic landscapes.

An exotic garden doesn't have to have flowers, but for most of us that dabble in this garden art, flowers are a valuable ingredient. There are no rules as to what flowering plants we include, but those that look most

The dramatic foliage of *Ricinus* and bananas contrasts well with big bright canna flowers suggesting the exuberance of exotic gardening.

appropriate have bright colours rather than pastel shades and will often have big showy blooms. Angel's trumpets, abutilons and dahlias are good flowering exotics that give a mass of colour. Probably the best examples are cannas, which not only have huge floppy flowers in brilliant colours but also large paddle leaves. A journalist I once knew described them as 'gladiolus gone bananas'!

We all have personal preferences in the garden, and it's this wonderful quirky subjectivity that makes so many gardens unique. Exotic gardening is no exception and, because it doesn't have clear rules, other exotic gardeners may include plants that I have omitted or wonder why I have enthused over some of my favourites. Some plants seem clear candidates for the exotic garden – such as cannas, bananas and palms – but there are others that are less clear. For

example, do we include hostas and ferns? Hostas have big bold leaves, many with bright colours, but to my mind they just seem like woodland plants along with ferns, which would appear happiest with primroses and bluebells, alongside a mossy stream. Am I guilty of plant prejudice maybe?

There is a certain fascination and challenge with exotic plants. In general they are not for the fainthearted – as we have seen most of them are big, bold and brash. Exotic gardening is somewhat exhibitionist. It says 'I'm pretending to be a jungle and I'm in the middle of the city!' For some of you, the origin of plants can be part of the fun, knowing that you have plants from probably all the continents of the world in your own back garden. 'Hey guys, do you know this agapanthus comes from South Africa?' And you can take pleasure from the fascinating uses of plants such as *Cyperus papyrus*, the original source of paper; *Agave tequilana*, the source of the drink tequila and *Canna edulis* used to make flour. The exotic garden encapsulates facts that will impress your visitors.

There is an element of make-believe in all exotic gardening, and those of us that explore it love the theatrical nature of creating a horticultural fantasy. Exotic gardening is fun, and many exotic landscapes will contain unusual and quirky plants as well as unexpected *objets d'art*. Over the years I have seen sculpture, ceramics, pieces of ruined architecture, skulls and even false dinosaur eggs!

Although most exotic gardeners have a very real sense of fun, they should not be dismissed lightly, as many of them are also highly skilled gardeners and plant collectors. They will have spent many years acquiring extensive collections of unusual plants and studying how to grow them, often in challenging climatic conditions. Their skill has enabled them to successfully grow plants that we wouldn't expect to find outside of the botanic garden or a heated greenhouse.

Hardiness and Climate

There is much debate about the influences of global warming on the species we can grow, and although there may be some climatic warming it is more likely that talk of global warming has influenced our thoughts and made gardeners more adventurous. For example, although for many years there have been

Some exotic gardeners prefer to create a more Mediterranean style with a fusion of pots containing exotic palms and other spiky plants.

Many of the exotic plants first imported to the United Kingdom in the nineteenth century would have been grown in fanciful greenhouses such as the Kibble Palace in Glasgow's Botanic Garden.

examples of mature olive trees in UK gardens, it is only in recent times that they have been more widely planted. Being a relatively small island, much of the UK is affected by the Gulf Stream, and coastal areas in particular have milder climates. Cities also have protected environments, and the combination of brick, concrete and tarmac all tend to hold urban heat. The larger cities such as London are almost frost-free and already have examples of tender trees such as *Acacia, Butia* and *Grevillea* not only surviving but thriving. Rural locations may not be so favourable, but south-facing slopes will tend to be warmer as will areas sheltered by existing tree cover. Gardens at the bottom of slopes can tend to act as frost pockets if cold air, which flows downwards, is trapped and cannot move away. Locations such as this should be avoided for exotic gardens.

This book is written from the perspective of the UK, but it is intended for use by gardeners in temperate regions of the world. The temperate latitudes of the globe lie between the tropics and the polar circles and include much of Europe and North America. Here the differences between summer and winter are mild rather than extreme. Temperate climates are not all the same though, and in large countries such as the

US there is considerable difference in the winter temperatures of some of the northern states such as Washington compared to the balmier climate of say California. Many other factors will also influence the local climate, such as various mountain ranges and coastal proximity.

Wherever your garden is located, growing exotic plants in a temperate climate is a great challenge for gardeners. Many exotic plants grow with great vigour in their home climates, and subjects such as *Bougainvillea, Strelitzia* and *Hibiscus* grow freely where there is warmth and abundant sunshine, in areas such as southern California. In warm climates, they are easy plants and are often taken for granted. But in temperate areas, such plants have to be cosseted, grown with skill and often various little tricks to make them perform well and create the illusion of an exotic garden in a temperate climate. Successfully growing bromeliads outside or getting bananas to fruit can nevertheless be very rewarding. Although we can make amends for low temperatures with extra protection or the use of glasshouses in the coldest weather, there is little we can do to compensate for the lack of sunshine. Sometimes plants fail, quite simply because the previous summer has not been warm or long enough for the wood to ripen. It is the really skilled gardeners that can make exotic plants thrive despite negative conditions. And it is this success, in the face of horticultural adversity, that is the reward for many exotic gardeners.

A Little History

Like all fashions, gardening trends come and go, and the current vogue for exotic planting is not entirely new. Exotic gardening as we know it was born in the late nineteenth century, particularly in the UK, as a development from the bedding craze.

Victorian Subtropicals

If we jump back to the mid-nineteenth century, we are in era of the great plant hunters and all the many wonderful new plant introductions that appeared in the Victorian era. Many of these came from warm climates and were initially grown in the great glasshouses of the big estates. The glass tax had been

repealed in 1845, and so glasshouses had become popular acquisitions for the landed gentry. Over time, gardeners experimented and tried planting these exotics outside for a summer display. Amazingly, many of these tender plants proved to grow quite satisfactorily in the temperate British summer, and so 'bedding out' was born. From this, carpet bedding developed, whereby low-growing foliage plants were used to create intricate patterns such as coats of arms and floral clocks.

The next stage was the use of more flamboyant foliage plants to create what became known as the 'subtropical garden', and it is this style that is the forerunner of our modern exotic garden. As the gardeners of the era explored the uses of foliage plants, they discovered that many of the more ostentatious foliage plants such as bananas, palms, and tree ferns would thrive outside rather than in the restricted confines of a hot house. Some of the earliest experiments took place in France, but it was very much in the UK that this style was pioneered. One of the most fashionable parks in the late nineteenth century was Battersea Park, and it is here that the head gardener, John Gibson experimented in 1868 with the first subtropical garden. The horticultural journals of the time report specimens of bananas up to 3m (10ft)

Battersea Park was one of the first public gardens to experiment using subtropical planting outside in the late nineteenth and early twentieth century as this early postcard shows.

tall, 'nearly superior to those seen in the natural habitats'. This was the first public subtropical garden and remained popular and widely visited right through to World War II, when it fell into decline. Fortunately, it has recently been restored.

Many other gardeners followed the fashion, and subtropical gardens were featured in private estates and public parks throughout the country. All sorts of hot house plants were tried outside with varying success – rubber plants, dracaenas, caladiums, ferns, coleus, castor oil plants, cannas and amazingly cannabis, grown purely for its ornamental foliage! This was particularly the age of the *Canna,* which rose from relative of obscurity to become an exceedingly popular plant, due mainly to the plant breeders of the era who transformed it from a tall leafy plant with small flowers to a more compact plant with huge flamboyant flowers. We will look at cannas in much more detail in Chapter 5, but it is relevant to emphasize that these became very important plants in Victorian subtropical displays. Although subtropical gardening was a development from bedding out, it was often demonstrated in a more informal way, with groups of exotics planted in sheltered dells amongst grass and other hardy planting.

William Robinson, one of the gardening writers of the era, was a great advocate of subtropical gardening and in 1871 published his book *The Subtropical Garden.* As well as enthusing over many of the plants that we will be talking about in this book, he outlined a number of practical procedures for ensuring the success of some of the more tender species. He spoke of raised beds with good drainage and the importance of warmth and shelter, which are just as relevant today as they were 150 years ago. It is an interesting book to peruse even now, although some of the plant names have changed beyond recognition. One does wonder what a *Canna rotundifolia-rubra-major* would look like, if it still exists. Fortunately plant naming has rationalized considerably since then.

During the early twentieth century, subtropical gardening along with elaborate bedding slowly slipped from favour, hastened by two World Wars and the inevitable changes in fashion. Gardening writers such as Gertrude Jekyll proposed a move towards a more natural cottage garden style, and the

Since exotic gardening became popular again in the late twentieth century, exotic show gardens such as this have appeared at many major flower shows.

herbaceous border was born. Then for over half a century sub-tropical plantings were almost forgotten, except for the occasional foliage bedding display that might be found in a traditional public park. Somewhere around the late 1980s there was a resurgence of interest in exotics, and since then the style has regained popularity.

The Exotic Renaissance

The late twentieth-century reawakening of interest may well be linked to various other factors. So many people now travel abroad for holidays, often to warm Mediterranean climates, where they enjoy landscapes filled with exotic plants. Gardeners return home to sad beds of bedraggled roses and, hey presto, the interest in exotic gardening is kindled. Climate change has also undoubtedly influenced the plants grown. Summers are often warmer and winters are generally milder, with the UK rarely experiencing extremes of cold. This has encouraged gardeners to be more adventurous and to gamble on plants with borderline hardiness such as bananas, tree ferns and palms.

Inevitably the nursery trade has developed to support this, and there is now no shortage of nurseries supplying exotic plants, including mature specimens of palms, bamboos, all manner of spikies and even aged, gnarled olive trees. Plants from many 'Mediterranean' areas such as South Africa, California, Australia, New Zealand and even South America have appeared in our garden centres and become surprisingly comfortable in our gardens. Many of these plants from Mediterranean areas are ideal for exotic gardens. As interest has grown, plant breeders have also responded, launching new cultivars or reintroducing old long-forgotten favourites.

Gardeners in many areas have discovered that they can grow and overwinter plants that would never have seemed hardy twenty years ago. This is one of the exciting aspects of global warming and offers us a whole host of new plants that gardeners would never have dreamed of growing outdoors in the past. Throughout this book there will be a number of plants noted as being borderline hardiness. These are the

gambles! All adventurous gardeners are horticultural speculators and love the challenge of trying something new. Some may not be successful, but others will be and may well end up becoming regular residents in not only exotic gardens but ordinary everyday gardens.

A gardener I once knew gardened in a chilly area on the outskirts of Manchester. She would comment, 'Never say a plant isn't hardy until you have killed it three times'. If she really wanted to grow something, she would play with it, moving it around, giving it a thick mulch or extra winter protection, until she managed to get it to grow successfully. In particular, each autumn she would visit a local jumble sale purchasing at the end of the event all the old woolly jumpers that nobody else wanted. These went home to her garden, where they were arranged over simple frameworks, protecting precious plants. Her garden in winter was quite a unique and colourful sight! But in this way she managed to grow a whole range of quite unexpected plants in this chilly area.

The Experts

Of the many people who have influenced this new wave of exotic gardening, two should be especially named, particularly because of the astonishing gardens they have created.

Will Giles

Over a period of twenty-five years or so, Will Giles has created the most astonishing exotic garden right in the middle of the city of Norwich. Visitors approach the garden either through a very narrow weedy alley or up an overgrown driveway, neither of which prepare you for the immaculate tropical oasis which suddenly opens out as you enter the garden. This one-acre site has the benefit of a south-facing slope and a mixture of established trees which give shelter.

Amongst the familiar, Will has planted a staggering range of exotic trees, shrubs and bamboos, to which each year he adds a psychedelic confection of tender exotics in brilliant colours. Huge towering bamboos jostle with giant bananas, lush cannas and some bright but very ordinary herbaceous perennials, which seem quite at home with their exotic bedfellows. In this garden you will find a mind-blowing array of plants, many of which you would not expect to find outdoors in the UK. Someone once accused Will of 'gardening with houseplants' and this is indeed part of what he does, but it should not be considered as a criticism, more a compliment to the flexibility with which he uses a wide range of exciting plants. After all, it was the Victorians who first took tropical hothouse plants and used them outside in the first nineteenth century subtropical displays. In many ways Will is repeating some of these experiments and very successfully.

As well as horticultural talents, Will is quite a builder. At the side of his house there is a towering grotto made of local flints, which constantly drips water from a high-level pond over the fronds of well-placed ferns into a murky pool at the base. Climbing the steps at the side of this feature, we are led to the arid garden set at the top of the steep slope behind the house. On a series of sunny terraces, Will has collected together a remarkable range of cacti and succulents, many of which have survived outside since 2008. The top of this garden is overlooked by a beautifully constructed, semi-ruined loggia, again built from local flints and finished with blue tiles. And if that isn't enough, as we make our way down the slope again, we are faced by an enormous tree house built into the framework of a huge oak tree. Standing inside this tree house is an awe-inspiring experience, looking out across the bananas, tree ferns and palms of the exotic garden to the roofscape of the city centre. The room itself is bisected by the branches of the tree, around which this quirky room is built. There can't be many individuals nowadays who garden in this way and are still building such fun garden follies.

Christopher Lloyd

No book on exotic gardening would be complete without highlighting the contribution made by the late Christopher Lloyd at Great Dixter in East Sussex. This historic garden has been created over many generations including contributions by great names such as Edwin Lutyens.

Christopher Lloyd, who died in 2006, was a horticulturalist of great repute and a renowned gardening writer. Some years ago he tired of the rather sad rose garden at Great Dixter, which was decimated by rose replant disease. With the help of Fergus Garrett, his head gardener, he set about creating an exotic garden. Traditionalists wept at the

Will Giles's tree house seems to float above a leafy jungle of bananas, palms and other lush plants in his amazing exotic garden in Norwich.

loss of the historic rose garden, but more adventurous gardeners were thrilled by his bold use of exotic plants. His garden includes most of the expected constituents – bananas, variegated grasses, cannas, palms, spiky leaved and architectural plants – all in a mix of well-ordered confusion.

In addition, the garden is punctuated with dahlias and threaded with *Verbena bonariensis*, two of Christopher's favourite plants. At a time when dahlias were often regarded as unfashionable, he embraced them, with all their voluptuous colour, and boldly used them in some very tongue-in-cheek colour schemes. By contrast, the verbena is a delicate plant in soft pinkish lavender, and he allowed this to seed itself throughout the exotic garden with total abandon. Some people may not be totally sure of all the effects that this plant creates here, but it is certainly distinctive. One memorable mix is the striking combination of the orange and bronze leafed *Canna* 'Wyoming', paired with that slender little red and yellow flowered climber, *Ipomoea lobata*. The two complement each other perfectly, but the haze of pinkish verbena which runs through the planting may make many gardeners cringe. Red, orange, yellow and pink together – the colours scream! But perhaps it is that unexpected additional colour which gives the basic combination its powerful punch.

Christopher Lloyd was renowned for his outspoken views, as well as his sometimes outrageous use of colour. I once commented to him that he obviously took great care over his colour schemes. He replied dismissively and somewhat mischievously that he put 'any old colours together'. I think we were both right, in that I'm sure that he did put all colours together in an experimental way, wondering what the results would be. Equally I'm sure that when he found successful combinations, he repeated them through-out the garden in the future.

At Great Dixter, Christopher Lloyd created an amazing confection of exotic flowers and foliage, threaded with his much loved *Verbena bonariensis*.

HARDY EXOTICS

Once described as 'lookalike exotics', these are the plants which have much of the exuberance and effect of tender exotics but are totally tough, hardy and permanent residents in our temperate jungles. Initially you might be tempted to think that they are the poor cousins or the less interesting plants in the garden, rather like low-calorie, sugar-free candy bars – useful but not very attractive. On the contrary, hardy exotics can not only be very valuable in the exotic garden but also provide stunning specimens in their own right. Many of these striking plants are full of colour and interest, entirely hardy and easy to grow.

Creating an Exotic Setting

There are many advantages to using exotics that are hardy. Using only tender exotics means the annual cost of replacing your display each summer would be excessive, whereas by using a proportion of permanent hardy exotics the cost is reduced. The time spent on looking after the garden will also be less as these tend to require less attention. Initially the financial outlay on hardy exotics can appear high. For example specimen bamboos, *Phormiums*, tree ferns or palms will all be expensive plants. But they will last for many years, gradually getting bigger and contributing increasingly to your display. The overall investment over a period of years will be considerably less than that of an annual replant of tender plants.

OPPOSITE PAGE: **Tree ferns and other hardy exotics create a lush effect, contrasting the formal decking and colourful seating in Jon Kelf's prize-winning modern exotic garden.**

Hardy exotics, whilst not being centre stage, will often provide a great deal of impact in an exotic garden because of their size and bulk. It is unlikely that any of the tender species you may plant, however attractive, will match the permanent plants for sheer size and certainly never in a single season. Well-established bamboos will easily exceed 5m (17ft), and eucalyptus quickly become trees. Even a mature plant of New Zealand flax can reach 3m (10ft) or more when in flower and will be a striking specimen. By planning carefully, you can mix hardy exotics in with the tender species, and viewing the end result you will not know what is hardy and what is tender.

When planning an exotic garden, it is wise to think in terms of planting hardy exotics at an early stage. This may sound terribly textbook boring – most of us probably want to get straight to the exciting tropical species that have caught our eye, either on holiday or at the garden centre – but nevertheless you will find it easier, and better aesthetically, if you begin by establishing the permanent structure. A framework of permanent hardy exotics will also give shelter to the tender species which you will later plant. Many tender species easily suffer from both wind damage and cold, and hardy exotics will help by softening wind and raising the overall temperature by a few degrees, often enough to encourage growth and avoid damage to the soft leaves of exotics.

Another advantage of using hardy species in an exotic garden is that it does give some winter interest. Most exotic gardens are summer spectaculars, and as soon as the first frost has passed, many species will have been damaged or already removed to a greenhouse for winter care. Having a framework of evergreens and structural hardy exotics does give some attraction in the colder months.

Exotics from Down Under

So many New Zealand plants seem to have strong shapes and bold foliage which fits perfectly with the exotic style. There are spiky *Phormiums, Astelias and Cordylines,* lacy *Pittosporums* and glossy-leaved *Griselinia.* The New Zealand climate can be described as similar to the UK, but nicer! It tends to be mild, with temperatures rarely below freezing and rarely above 30°C (86°F). As such, it is not surprising that many New Zealand plants thrive in the UK. Following the brutally hard UK winter of 2009–2010 when temperatures plummeted to their lowest for many years, it is amazing how many New Zealand plants survived almost unscathed. In the author's small garden, many phormiums, pittosporums, coloured-leaved cordylines, olearias and *Corokia* have all come through almost undamaged. Phormiums are exhibiting broken leaves, from the sheer weight of snow, but are otherwise unscathed.

If you were going to invent a new best-selling plant you might want it to have a great shape, be evergreen with year round interest and available in a wide range of colours. Well, the *Phormiums* fit the bill almost exactly. They make fabulous architectural plants, with a strong shape that is effective almost from the day of planting and can be found in many almost luminous colours.

The basic green-leaved *Phormium tenax* is itself a striking architectural plant, making huge leafy clumps growing to 2m (7ft) or more. Once established they will often flower with even taller elegant spikes of small brownish red flowers. The skeletal seedheads which follow will usually hang on the plants, remaining ornamental until the next year. The basic species is quite tough and will survive a certain amount of frost, although it does not like poor drainage or prolonged freezing. The purple-leaved form 'Purpureum' is almost as tall and just as hardy.

There are, then, many colourful-leaved *Phormium* cultivars with varying hardiness. Favourites include 'Yellow Wave' with green foliage striped with yellow, and the sooty-coloured 'Platt's Black', which is a quite compact cultivar. You will find many cultivars in shades of pink, red and purple, such as 'Dazzler' and 'Sundowner'. The coloured-leaved types tend to be shorter in stature than the plain green species and so can often be positioned towards the front of the border, where their shape and colours can be best appreciated.

Phormium 'Yellow Wave' growing in a novel container made from old tyres, contrasting with blue agapanthus and a yellow ceramic ball.

Some of the coloured-leaved cultivars tend to lose the intensity of colour in their foliage after a few years. When this happens, try cutting back brutally hard to a stump around 20cm (8in) tall. Feed well, keep moist, mulch generously, and you will be rewarded with a flush of fresh, new, brilliantly-coloured leaves. It's a simple way of rejuvenating old plants.

Astelia chatamica 'Silver Spear' has gained popularity in recent years and is now readily available. It comes from New Zealand but is proving to be almost totally hardy. The spiky foliage is soft green on its upper surface and a silvery white underneath. Its architectural shape makes it useful as a low-level accent plant. Although it does occasionally flower, the blooms are not attractive and should be removed. There is a lovely muted coppery bronze version, called 'Westland', which is equally attractive.

Despite its name, *Cordyline australis* also originates from New Zealand. It is commonly called the cabbage palm, although there is no relationship to palms or cabbages. The basic green cordyline has a loose spiky shape, with narrow strap-like leaves radiating from a central point, giving nicely feathered plants. Cordylines have been widely used in bedding and as container plants for many years, but it is only recently with our milder winters that they have been able to grow to mature specimens which become small multi-branched wild west-looking trees. Although primarily grown for their foliage, they flower when mature, with huge clusters of white, sickly-sweet scented flowers. The bronze-leaved form 'Atropurpurea' is also virtually hardy and will grow into a substantial specimen. In recent years quite a number of attractive coloured-leaved forms have been bred, such as the cream and green variegated 'Torbay Dazzler', the vivid and aptly named 'Pink Stripe' and the moody 'Black Tower'. Most of these fancy coloured forms tend to be far less hardy so should be considered as temporary summer additions to our exotic garden.

Then there are the *Pittosporums*. These are evergreen shrubs with small glossy leaves in green, bronze and various combinations of silver and gold. They make upright bushy plants, some growing to as much as 4m (13ft). Used as background plants in an exotic garden, they are much tougher than many

This simple but striking group of hardy exotics features bamboos, a flowering phormium and a purple cordyline underplanted with *Corydalis lutea.*

gardening books would suggest. The small foliage is a superb contrast against large-leaved exotics. The basic green *Pittosporum tennuifolium* is quite vigorous and will make a small tree not unlike *Ficus nitida,* widely planted in warm climates. The variegated types are generally more compact. Both 'Irene Paterson', with its white speckled leaves and 'Garnettii', with its white margins and pink splashes, are said to be tender but thrive in temperate areas, as does 'Tandara Gold'. In spring they all produce a mass of tiny deep maroon flowers that would go unnoticed except for their sweet chocolaty scent. The shortest of all is 'Tom Thumb', which makes a small bun-shaped plant about a metre in height. It is quite distinct in being one of the few evergreen plants with purple foliage.

The glossy-leaved, evergreen *Griselinias* also come from New Zealand. The simple green *G. littoralis* makes a valuable background or screening plant and is salt tolerant for maritime areas but is easily upstaged by the variegated types for garden display. Look out for the cultivars 'Dixon's Cream' or 'Bantry Bay', both of which have excellent golden colourings.

Bamboos

Bamboos are such useful plants in the exotic garden. They are related to grasses but have a woody framework. Bamboos have a bad reputation for being invasive – and indeed some will take over the garden if you let them loose – but these are in the minority. Bamboos fall into two categories, either clump-forming or running. Generally it is better to avoid the running types in a small garden. Nevertheless there are some runners which are very beautiful and you may want to try growing them, but monitor their spread to prevent them from becoming a nuisance.

Bamboo plants are strikingly architectural, with strong vertical shapes softened by delicate evergreen foliage held on small side shoots from the main canes.

Many have beautifully coloured canes which remain attractive for a number of years. *Phyllostachys nigra* is well known as the black bamboo and is a well-behaved clumping bamboo. Few people can resist *Phyllostachys vivax* 'Aurocaulis' with its vivid banana-yellow canes striped with green. Unfortunately it is a spreading bamboo, so it should be watched and where necessary controlled. It has the curious habit of sending up lone canes some distance from the mother plant, sometimes even in the middle of an adjacent lawn.

Bamboos can be both a nuisance and also strikingly beautiful. If you want to restrain any of the running bamboos, either plant them in a large container plunged in the ground with the base removed or enclose the whole clump with a root barrier. Purpose-made root barriers are basically very tough but flexible polythene sheeting which can be sunk in the soil around individual plants.

A few bamboos are variegated, such as the abominably named *Hibanobambusa tranquillans* 'Shiroshima'. It has large glossy leaves with striking creamy variegations and grows to about 2m (7ft). *Pleioblastus auricomus* is not much more than a groundcover plant, but its velvety golden foliage makes it well worth growing as an understory plant.

With most bamboos, the colourful canes are partially hidden behind a fuzz of foliage on the small side shoots. To further enhance the effect of bamboos, trim off the lower side shoots cleanly back to the main canes using a pair of secateurs. It's a slow job but they do not re-grow, so you do not have to repeat the job, although you will need to deal with any new canes each year. For the health of the plant, you must leave some foliage and so never trim them for more than 50 per cent of their overall height. With almost all bamboos this is quite adequate, leaving a small thicket of beautiful glossy green, black or yellow canes.

Bamboos such as this *Fargesia* provide excellent hardy and architectural background plants in this exotic garden.

Everyday Exotics

As well as the particular groups we have already described, there are many other individual plants that can be used as hardy exotics. One 'must have' plant for the exotic garden is *Tetrapanax papyrifer*, originating from Taiwan but seemingly hardy in most temperate locations. It produces huge palmate green leaves, sometimes over 60cm (2ft) across, on a handsome plant, eventually reaching over 3m (10ft) when mature. It has the surprising habit of sending up suckers quite some distance from the main plant, although it is rarely a nuisance. It is semi-evergreen and in a mild winter will retain a proportion of its foliage through to the spring. There is a selection called 'Rex', which has slightly larger even more impressive leaves.

Fatsia japonica has large glossy green leaves like chubby hands and is totally evergreen, so makes a good background plant. Its relative *Aralia elata* makes tall prickly stems, at the top of which there is a mop of finely divided foliage. It's easy to grow, tough and suckers discreetly, which means that in time you get a small thicket of plants. As well as the plain green form there are two variegated types, with gold and white variegated foliage respectively. They are much slower growing than the green-leaved species but produce huge beautifully marked leaves which are quite spectacular. Unfortunately they have to be grafted, which means that they are very tricky plants to produce and the cost will be high.

The classical fig, *Ficus carica*, makes a good inclusion amongst other hardy exotics. It has bold foliage with an interesting shape, and given time it will also fruit. However it is deciduous and so its value is really

ABOVE: **Removing the sideshoots on bamboos such as this *Phyllostachys aurea* reveals the striking and colourful culms in all their glory.**

RIGHT: ***Tetrapanax papyrifer* is probably one of the most dramatic of hardy exotic plants, although it needs plenty of space to develop its full potential.**

Once established, *Acacia dealbata* **will make an attractive medium-size tree with silvery foliage and regular spring mimosa blossom.**

summer only. Another deciduous plant well worth trying is the purple-leaved Judas tree, *Cercis canadensis* 'Forest Pansy'. This makes a large shrub or small tree covered with large, rounded purple leaves. Locate this plant in an open situation, where the sun will shine down through the leaves, and it becomes quite magnificent.

Exotic trees

Trees are valuable in any landscape, as they give height, presence and maturity to a garden. The many species of *Eucalyptus* from Australia are very useful here. Most have silver foliage and are easy fast-growing plants. *Eucalyptus gunnii*, the cider gum is

probably the most readily available. Like most eucalyptus, the juvenile leaves are round, but as the tree grows towards maturity the shape of the leaf becomes more elongated. Because of their speed of growth, eucalyptus can become nuisance trees quite quickly, but they respond very well to hard pruning. Most eucalyptus can be cut hard, either to ground level or to a short framework, and they will readily sprout fresh growth. This new growth usually bears the juvenile foliage, similar to when the plant was young.

Acacias are another valuable group of exotic-looking trees, many of which originate from Australia. Out of the many species there are a few which are reliably hardy. Probably the most familiar is *Acacia dealbata*, known by many as the florist's mimosa. It seems to be reliably hardy in temperate areas, growing vigorously to provide a medium-size tree. Acacias bear masses of small yellow powder puff-like flowers in spring. The delicate flowers and foliage contrast well with bolder foliage and flowers.

You can use pruning to encourage exotics to produce a more suitable shape for the garden. Stooling is an old but effective technique for encouraging certain plants to grow extremely vigorously and produce huge leaves, which can be quite spectacular within the exotic garden. *Paulownia tomentosa*, the foxglove tree, responds very well to this treatment. If left to grow naturally this makes a large tree, with medium-size leaves and eventually blue flowers. Alternatively each spring you can hard prune this plant either down to ground level or to a stump, say 1.8m (6ft) above the ground. Feed the plant well with a general fertilizer. After growth starts, you should reduce the stems to say, three to five, and this gives maximum leaf size whilst still maintaining a nicely shaped plant. Quite quickly you will be rewarded with strong shoots and huge tea tray sized, round leaves. It is very much a showstopper in any exotic garden. If you want a really startling result, remove all but one of the resulting shoots and allow this to grow alone. By the end of the season, you will have a plant that may reach to 5m (16ft) or more, stretching up to the clouds! The Indian bean tree, and particularly the gold leaf form, *Catalpa bignonioides* 'Aurea', also responds particularly well to

ABOVE: **Hard pruning of *Paulownia tomentosa*, known as stooling, encourages vigorous growth with huge tea tray sized green leaves.**

this treatment. Over the years some gardeners have tried other species, including shrubs such as *Rhus typhina*, *Cotinus coggygria* 'Royal Purple', *Corylus maxima* 'Purpurea', coloured-leaved forms of *Sambucus* such as 'Sutherland Gold' and 'Black Lace'. *Ailanthus altissima* and of course *Eucalyptus* will produce strong growth and lush foliage.

One of the classic Mediterranean trees which is amazingly hardy is the fruiting olive, *Olea europaea*. A hot summer is needed for fruit to be produced and ripen, but even without this the soft grey foliage of the tree is attractive. In recent years, a market has developed in importing from abroad established trees that have wonderful gnarled trunks full of character. The top growth of these specimens will have been cut back hard for transport but will grow again quickly, giving the effect of old mature olive trees. Such trees are usually quite expensive and should be used as focal points on their own, maybe set in grass or gravel, where their full beauty can be appreciated.

BELOW: **The dark foliage of *Cercis canadensis* 'Forest Pansy' looks best when positioned so that the sun can shine through the rich ruby red leaves.**

Other trees that can be used in the exotic garden include the various different types of *Robinia pseudoacacia,* such as the golden-leaved 'Frisia'. Somewhat similar, *Sophora japonica,* the Japanese pagoda tree, is also fast growing with lush pinnate foliage. *Koelreuteria paniculata,* the golden rain tree looks quite exotic with jagged foliage and brilliant yellow flowers. Some of the larger-leaved pines such as *Pinus coulteri* or *Pinus motezumae* are quite fun as are other unusual conifers such as the weeping *Chamaecyparis nootkatensis* 'Pendula' or the delicate *Cupressus cashmeriana.* The hardy palm, *Trachycarpus fortunei* will eventually reach tree proportions, but it is painfully slow and mature specimens are expensive.

Hardy Climbers

Climbers are useful in any garden and, as the space above your plot is free, why not use it? You may just like the idea of climbers scrambling through other plants in true jungle fashion or you may have walls,

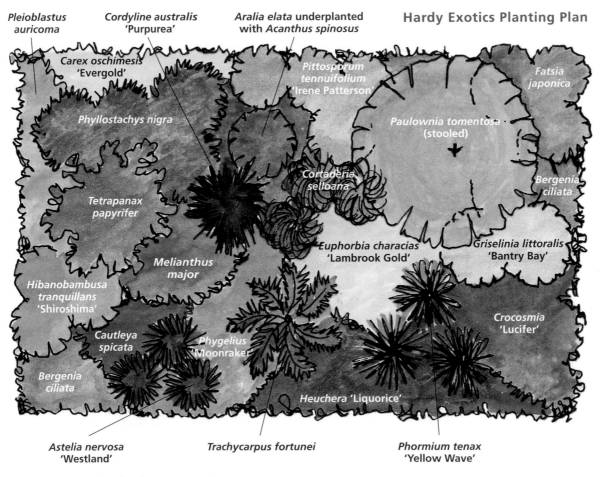

Hardy Exotics Planting Plan

Pleioblastus auricoma

Cordyline australis 'Purpurea'

Aralia elata underplanted with *Acanthus spinosus*

Carex oschimesis 'Evergold'

Pittosporum tennuifolium 'Irene Patterson'

Fatsia japonica

Phyllostachys nigra

Paulownia tomentosa (stooled)

Cortaderia selloana

Bergenia ciliata

Tetrapanax papyrifer

Euphorbia characias 'Lambrook Gold'

Griselinia littoralis 'Bantry Bay'

Melianthus major

Hibanobambusa tranquillans 'Shiroshima'

Crocosmia 'Lucifer'

Cautleya spicata

Phygelius 'Moonraker'

Bergenia ciliata

Heuchera 'Liquorice'

Astelia nervosa 'Westland'

Trachycarpus fortunei

Phormium tenax 'Yellow Wave'

This bold scheme relies entirely on low-maintenance hardy exotics with many different types of contrasting and variegated foliage such as the *Tetrapanax,* purple cordyline, *Griselinia* and pampas grass. Summer colour is provided by *Crocosmia, Cautleya* and *Euphorbia.* Height is provided by a stooled *Paulownia* and a group of black bamboo. The centrepiece of the border is the hardy palm, *Trachycarpus fortunei,* which will in time become a small tree.

Crocosmia 'Lucifer' and *Hemerocallis* 'Nefertiti', seen here with a bronze *Phormium*, are both bold and bright enough to use in exotic plantings.

trellises or archways that need covering in a more formal way. One of the most exotic-looking foliage climbers is that relative of the grapevine, *Vitis coignetiae*. Throughout the summer it produces an abundance of huge leaves which turn a rich orange-red as the summer fades. The golden-leaved form of the common hop, *Humulus lupulus* 'Aureus' is also another lush summer climber. It will make four or more metres of growth each summer, all covered in rich buttery yellow foliage. Being an herbaceous perennial, it all dies down in the winter and so starts again from ground level the next spring, rarely becoming unsightly or a nuisance.

For flowers, try the tongue trippingly named *Campsis tagliabuana* 'Madame Galen', a relative of the Indian bean tree. Once established, it will produce wonderful clusters of waxy tropical-looking red flowers which are well worth waiting for. Abutilons are really shrubs rather than climbers, but some, such as *Abutilon megapotanicum, A. x milleri* or 'Patrick Synge' are lax enough to scramble through other exotics. Most passion flowers are tender, but the blue-flowered *Passiflora caerulea* is hardy, as is the white form 'Constance Elliot'. The golden-leaved form of *Jasminum officinale* has white scented flowers as well as delicate golden variegated foliage. It is vigorous and will scramble through other shrubs with abandon to the point at which it may need severe pruning. 'Fiona Sunrise' has pure gold leaves and is somewhat less unruly. *Aristolochia macrophylla* is a twining climber with large lush leaves, attractive as a foliage plant. It is rather shy in flowering but when it does it produces bizarre, fleshy-looking flowers in shades of brown – decidedly sci-fi but great fun in an exotic garden.

Exotic Fruits

Most exotic fruits require warmer climates than we can offer to produce viable fruit, although some are worth growing for their ornamental value and as talking points. One of the hardiest of all exotic fruits is the loquat, *Eriobotrya japonica*, which makes a large shrub or small tree with dark, prominently veined, evergreen foliage. In good summers, white flowers may be followed by edible yellow fruits. Kiwi fruits, *Actinidia deliciosa*, can also be grown and fruited successfully in temperate areas and this vigorous leafy scrambler is fine for the exotic garden. The cultivar 'Jenny' is self fertile and should produce reasonable crops of fruit. Figs have already been mentioned and these are of course reliable fruiters in temperate climates with decidedly exotic foliage.

Herbaceous Exotics

I guess most of you will think of herbaceous perennials in the context of cottage gardens and traditional herbaceous borders. Well, ignore the well-behaved dowagers such as delphiniums, lupins and hollyhocks and discover some of the herbaceous extroverts which are flamboyant enough for any exotic garden.

Probably one of the most dramatic is *Gunnera manicata*. It can make as much as 3m (10ft) of growth in a season and has enormous rugged green leaves that are big enough to shelter under on a rainy day. The stocky flower spikes are buried underneath the foliage and contain hundreds of tiny individual flowers, fascinating but generally hidden from view so we really grow it for its foliage alone. It prefers a moist situation, preferably next to a pond or stream, where it will perform to its maximum potential. The foliage will collapse in the autumn, with the first frost. As the crown can be somewhat tender, pile up the dead brown leaves over the growing point for winter protection.

The genus *Euphorbia* is a large group of plants, most of which have greyish foliage and spikes bearing showy yellow bracts. These valuable architectural plants are sub-shrubs, but they are treated very much like herbaceous plants. Some of the best are the various forms of *Euphorbia characias* subsp *wulfenii*, such as 'Lambrook Gold' and 'John Tomlinson'. Both make nicely rounded balls of grey foliage which are topped with dramatic spikes of limey yellow each spring. You may also like to try *Euphorbia mellifera*, with bright apple green leaves highlighted with a clear white line through the centre of each leaf. In early summer it produces small brownish flowers which are richly scented with honey. Although not a dramatic plant it is nevertheless quite appealing.

Euphorbias look good planted next to purple foliage such as *Heuchera* 'Palace Purple', which brings us to another group of herbaceous perennials. The heucheras have rather shot to fame in recent years with a flurry of new and interesting cultivars. Although they do flower with small spikes of delicate either pink or white flowers, it is for their evergreen foliage that we generally grow them. They make low mounds of somewhat crinkly leaves in numerous jewel-like colours, making them excellent permanent ground-cover under tall plants. 'Palace Purple' was one of the first of the new wave, and that has now been joined by numerous others, some with coppery orange leaves such as 'Crème Brûlée', limey greens including 'Key Lime Pie', many more purples, and some almost black such as 'Obsidian'. Well worth including in the exotic garden, either as groundcover plants or with other exotics at the front of the display.

The bergenias, commonly known as elephant's ears, are 'love 'em or hate 'em' plants. They are tough as anything, with large, glossy leaves which fit nicely into the exotic style. One favourite is *Bergenia ciliata*, which originates from Nepal. It has huge dinner plate sized leaves which are covered with tiny white hairs. Although it is said to be tender, it can be found in sheltered spots in many gardens. Bergenias look particularly good against the narrow foliage and vertical stems of bamboos or grasses.

Later on we will mention the tender aroids, but here we can include the large-flowered arum lilies, botanically known as *Zantedeschia*. The most familiar is *Z. aethiopica*, which bears large white spathes, often thought of as funeral lilies. They prefer a damp, slightly shady location or can be grown in shallow water at the side of a pool. There is a limey green version called 'Green Goddess' and a pale pink cultivar called 'Kiwi Blush'. All of these are tough, hardy and easy to grow.

Acanthus also produces lovely lush green foliage, immortalized on Greek architecture. *Acanthus mollis* is the common species, but *A. spinosus* has finer, more delicate foliage. Both produce stately spikes of off-white flowers with vicious spines. They resent disturbance, so plant them and leave well alone. From South Africa we get the genus *Agapanthus*, which should also be left undisturbed to encourage their giant spidery globes of blue or white flowers. Although they can be planted out in a dry, well-drained sunny site, they do exceedingly well in pots, and when pot-bound are more likely to flower freely. In addition there are many bold and colourful herbaceous perennials such as *Crocosmia, Rudbeckia, Helenium, Hemerocallis* and *Kniphofia* that can be used.

Exotic Grasses

Ornamental grasses are another vast group of great garden plants, many of which are excellent candidates for the exotic garden. Most are hardy perennials, so they are easy plants to grow and permanent contributors to our exotic display. Their narrow leaves contrast well with bolder foliage.

Do try some of the taller *Miscanthus* such as 'Cabaret' or 'Cosmopolitan', both of which are variegated. They are totally hardy and grow to about 1.5m (5ft) each year but die back to the ground in the winter. The pampas grasses are also tall and much maligned as being unfashionable, but they are excellent garden plants which fit well into exotic schemes. *Cortaderia selloanna* is the best-known and most vigorous, making a huge sinuous mound of narrow green foliage topped by towering creamy blooms each autumn. There is an excellent golden-leaved version called a 'Gold Band' and some silver variegated cultivars which are worth trying.

At the other end of the scale there is a compact but vibrant golden groundcover grass called *Hakonechloa*

Although totally hardy, the water-loving *Zantedeschia* 'Kiwi Blush' has lush exotic foliage and unusual early summer flowers.

macra 'Aureola' with soft trailing foliage striped in gold. A new introduction called 'All Gold' has pure golden-yellow foliage and looks great against vivid purples, such as the dark *Heuchera* 'Plum Pudding'.

Hardy Exotics Only?

So do you need tropicals when you can have bamboos, spiky foliage, big bold leaves and colourful climbers all without a greenhouse in sight? In the next chapter we will look particularly at foliage and find that there are also some hardy palms, tree ferns and bananas that thrive outside. Amongst the huge range of hardy exotic plants you will find not only plenty of candidates for the skeleton of an exotic garden but enough to create your own exotic landscape without any tender plants.

EXOTIC CLASSICS

Amongst the many fast-growing plants, with huge leaves, and striking shapes, there are a few classic exotics that immediately conjure up the atmosphere of a tropical landscape. These are the real 'jungley' exotics – bananas with their huge paddle leaves, palms with their distinct shapes, tree ferns with their soft lush foliage and the prehistoric-looking cycads.

Bananas

For sheer foliar exuberance, bananas have to top the bill. In recent years a number of species have become increasingly available through nurseries and garden centres, and adventurous gardeners have found them to be rewarding plants to grow. Bananas aren't for the faint hearted, however. Their huge, floppy leaves are glossy and showy and tend to take centre stage, even in an exotic garden.

To use them successfully in a planting scheme, you need to appreciate and use their essentially extrovert and brassy appearance. Mix them with mild-mannered neighbours such roses and delphiniums, and the bananas will look like thugs. Instead, contrast bananas with bold foliage such as *Fatsia japonica, Euphorbia wulfenii, Phormium tenax* 'Yellow Wave' or *Sambucus* 'Black Lace'. All are permanent hardy species, so with careful arrangement the evergreens

OPPOSITE PAGE: **Musa basjoo, the hardy banana makes an impressive clump of vigorous foliage and a considerable exotic statement within a few years.**

such as *Fatsia* and *Phormium* can at least partially hide the banana when wrapped for winter.

Under windy conditions, banana leaves tend to be shredded, particularly in late summer, so some shelter is valuable. Despite this, the cut foliage has a sort of tropical ruggedness that is not unattractive. Compliment them with other bold foliage such as *Melianthus* and add some summer colour from dahlias, cannas and coleus to give a stunning display.

Hardy Bananas

Undoubtedly the most familiar and easiest banana to grow is *Musa basjoo*, sometimes called the hardy banana. It is a native of China but grows well in temperate climates and, given a sheltered spot and a warm summer, it can make a spectacular plant with huge 2m (7ft) long green leaves. It responds to generous watering and feeding, making a real statement that screams exotic in any garden.

Like all bananas, *Musa basjoo* is actually a suckering herbaceous perennial, despite its impressive 'trunk'. This is not a true stem but is made up of leaf sheaths wrapped together, a bit like an onion. The actual growing point is at ground level, hidden within this false stem. This means that although the top growth is not frost hardy, the underground rootstock will usually survive overwinter and send up new shoots from ground level. A thick mulch will ensure this regeneration.

Some gardeners have developed ingenious methods for wrapping the false stems of M. basjoo with some sort of winter protection, to encourage them to survive the winter (*see* page 84). New growth the next year then starts from the top of the 'stem',

The recently introduced *Musa sikimensis* has subtle purple tints to the leaves, seen here with *Phormium tenax* 'Atropurpurea' and *Arundo donax* 'Variegata'.

and a more impressive plant is created instantly. In this way some gardeners have achieved banana 'trees', quite substantial in size, complete with flowers and fruit. Although the fruit on this banana is full of black seeds and unpalatable, it's still nevertheless impressive to boast fruiting bananas in your back garden.

Another old timer, *Musa sikimensis,* was first discovered and named in the nineteenth century. It has only recently become more available in the nursery trade. It is similar to *M. basjoo* and produces enormous, dramatic leaves, often with a distinct purple flush on the undersides. It can be variable and it is worth looking for a good, well-coloured form of this plant when purchasing. Its hardiness is similar to *M. basjoo* and is therefore treated and protected in a similar way.

Tender Bananas

Some bananas must be overwintered in a frost-free greenhouse and just bedded out for summer display. The Victorians were very fond of *Ensete ventricosum*, correctly known as the Abyssinian or Ethiopian banana. Its huge green paddle-like leaves made perfect centrepieces for their elaborate bedding displays, and it can be just as spectacular in an exotic garden today. It is easily grown from seed and makes an impressive plant in a short space of time.

If exotic gardening is theatre, then the purple banana is one of the stars, a true prima donna, needing centre stage and a little cosseting. Provide its needs, and it will give a show-stopping performance. To give it its full name, *E. ventricosa* 'Maurelii', the Red

Ensete ventricosa 'Maurelii' is probably the most dramatic of all bananas with rich purple foliage, growing several metres tall.

For real edible bananas, *Musa acuminata* 'Dwarf Cavendish' must be grown, but ideally it needs to remain in a warm greenhouse to fruit properly.

Abyssinian Banana is undoubtedly the most spectacular of all bananas. It is a vigorous and statuesque plant, with rich ruby red foliage. Many garden centres and nurseries will stock it in summer.

It is an excellent garden plant and will grow well in a patio tub or planted out as a border plant. The huge purple paddle leaves appearing from amongst other foliage at the back of the border have instant 'wow' effect. A two or three-year-old plant at 2m (7ft) or more is a splendid sight, although the vivid colouring is at its most intense with younger plants. Being a tender plant this banana is often best associated with other summer ephemerals. Plant it as the centrepiece with the silver foliage of *Melianthus major*, variegated grasses such as *Miscanthus sinensis* 'Cosmopolitan' and the purple fountain grass, *Pennisetum setaceum* 'Rubrum'. Add *Iresine* 'Brilliantissimum', dark 'Arabian Night' dahlias and richly coloured coleus 'Henna'.

You may also come across *Musella lasiocarpa* in garden centres. This has greyish green leaves and an inverted cone shape. It can be planted out for summer or grown as a specimen in a small tub. As it does not grow too big, it is not difficult to transfer it to a frost-free greenhouse for the winter. Over a period of two or three years it will make a chunky plant no more than a metre or so in height with many suckers, which can be readily detached and grown on as very desirable gifts. The parent plant then gives its star performance by flowering with huge yellow, lotus-like flowers, which last for many months.

If you want 'real' bananas try *Musa acuminata* 'Dwarf Cavendish'. This makes a compact banana plant that is not only ornamental but produces edible and very sweet fleshed fruits. It can be planted out for summer display but really needs a heated glasshouse with a winter temperature of at least 10°C (50°F) to grow and fruit. It is quite possible to grow this to fruiting stage in a conservatory and be the envy of the neighbourhood.

Like all bananas, after flowering and fruiting, the main stem will start to decline and will eventually die. For tidiness, remove this to ground level and keep the plant well-fed and watered. New shoots will develop from the base and can either be left to grow on as a clump or separated and replanted individually.

Palms

These exotics have distinctive foliage and a strong shape which is very evocative of warm climates, steamy jungles and sunshine holidays, so naturally you will want to include some in your exotic garden. Although many are genuine tropical plants and not really feasible in a temperate climate, there are some which can be successfully grown in cooler conditions. All are architectural plants with a characteristic shape, which suggests that they should usually be planted as accent plants in a key location, rather than mixed in with background planting.

Palm foliage is normally green but may be displayed in a number of different ways, sometimes categorized

This exotic garden features a range of spiky plants and palms, including *Brahea armata*, the Mexican blue palm and a range of spiky agaves.

as fan, feather, fishtail or entire. The fan and feather palms are the commonest ones for us to consider in temperate climates. Many have distinct trunks, often slender, very tall and extremely flexible, being able to withstand high winds. Others are clumping, producing a small group of short trunks. When planted as specimens in a lawn, they are especially effective when the sun shines and you get the added bonus of beautiful shadow patterns cast by their fronds.

The most readily available of all palms for use in temperate areas is *Trachcarpus fortunei,* otherwise known as the Chusan palm. It was introduced to the UK in 1848 by Robert Fortune, whose name it bears. The original tree can still be seen at Kew Gardens, and places such as the Abbotsbury Subtropical Gardens exhibit some wonderful old specimens with towering trunks, demonstrating its longevity and hardiness in the sometimes tough UK climate. It forms a single trunk, covered with a mass of shaggy, fibrous hairs and topped with a head of fan-shaped leaves. It is very hardy but also slow-growing, so you will either have to be very patient or buy a mature specimen to get an immediate effect.

Chamaerops humilis, the Mediterranean fan palm, is also readily available from nurseries and garden centres. It is a compact clump-forming palm that grows no taller than a man and so is very suitable for a small garden. It is totally hardy in temperate conditions, though beware of its sharp prickles when handling. Some specialist nurseries may offer *Chamaerops humilis* 'Cerifera', the blue Mediterranean fan palm which, as the name suggests, has wonderful steely blue leaves. Growers suggest that it is as hardy as the plain species.

As well as palms that are reliably hardy, there are others that are becoming available and may well be worth trying in temperate conditions. As with any other plants of borderline hardiness, you will need to find a sheltered location, with good drainage. In the early years after planting, it may well be worth wrapping up precious palms with fleece, straw or sacking during the winter months.

Another blue-leaved palm worth trying is *Brahea armata,* the Mexican blue fan palm. A well grown healthy plant of this species makes a striking

Trachcarpus fortunei, the Chusan palm is slow-growing but totally hardy, and contrasts well with the equally hardy grass *Miscanthus sinensis* 'Variegata'.

specimen, with big waxy fans of steely blue leaves. However it is not as hardy as the others we have mentioned so far and can be temperamental, so plant it in a sheltered location and cosset it over the first few winters with some extra fleece as protection.

Phoenix canariensis, the Canary Island date palm, is well known from holidays abroad as a towering tree. In temperate areas, it is rarely seen as tree size specimens but is nevertheless tolerant of a certain amount of cold. It is a vigorous plant and a young well-established specimen can be three or more metres wide, so allow plenty of space when planting. Some adventurous growers have also had some

The lush foliage of of *Dicksonia antarctica*, the Tasmanian tree fern makes an impressive sight, creating an instant exotic atmosphere.

success with *Washingtonia robusta*, the Mexican fan palm, which is said to be hardy down to –4°C (25°F).

You may also like to look for the Jelly Palm, *Butia capitata*, which comes from Brazil but is nevertheless quite tough and fairly hardy. It makes a single knobbly trunk, topped with beautiful blue-green feather-like leaves that curve downwards. There are many other palms that are offered by specialist nurseries, with certain levels of hardiness, and if you like the idea of palms in an exotic garden then it's well worth trying some of the others on offer.

Under temperate conditions you will generally see relatively short young palms which will have a wide spreading habit but not the typical stature given by a trunk. To create more of a 'palm tree' effect, plant in a tall contemporary container or something simple like a 2m (6ft) section of aluminium ducting. Don't attempt to make this look like a palm stem but just enjoy the effect of palm fronds waving overhead. If grown in tubs or planters the root system will be more exposed being above ground and will need winter protection.

Tree Ferns

This is another large group of very exotic-looking foliage plants. These are ancient and primitive plants that date back to the Jurassic and Cretaceous periods. It is reasonable to suggest that dinosaurs walked around under the shade of tree ferns, and so these are very much the right plants to give our exotic garden a real jungle atmosphere. There are many species, which come from tropical and subtropical parts of the world, but in practice those available in nurseries are quite limited. Until recently they were almost unseen in temperate gardens, except those with a very favourable climate such Heligan in Cornwall. This garden was left untended for around seventy years until rediscovered in the 1990s, and amongst all the brambles and weeds were some amazing surviving plants including tree ferns.

In recent years, plants of *Dicksonia antarctica* have become increasingly available, and you can find them in many garden centres and in gardens throughout the UK. This is another example of an exotic plant that is becoming a familiar constituent of landscapes. They have hairy trunks topped by enormous heads of long fronds, a metre or more in length. When well established and in full growth they make handsome plants. Although you can purchase them as growing plants, complete with a head of foliage, they are more easily and economically bought as a dormant section of trunk with a growing point. They're usually sold by size, so small chunks will cost considerably less than a two-metre section of trunk, which when established becomes an instant tree. They are particularly rewarding, as a full head of new fronds will emerge and expand over just a few weeks.

Buy the biggest tree ferns you can afford, because they really are exceptional plants. If you are planting a group, they look most effective with plants of different sizes grouped together. Like most ferns, they prefer light shade rather than full sunshine, which will be likely to scorch the foliage, so plant them amongst other taller species. *Dicksonia antarctica* has proved amazingly hardy and in milder winters will retain most of its foliage to the next season. Young plants grow well in containers and can be used for patio display until planted out.

You might also like to try the slightly smaller *Dicksonia fibrosa* or the multi-stemmed *D. squarrosa*, both of which are reasonably hardy. *Cyathea australis* may well be successful and also *C. dealbata*.

Cycads – Leafy Dinosaurs

These curious plants are often mistaken for palms or tree ferns but aren't related to either. They are nevertheless fascinating plants, as they also date from the Jurassic period and as such are some of the few remaining prehistoric plants. They have huge, finely divided leaves that appear very similar to feather palms. Most however, are plants of short stature, with at the most, a squat dumpy trunk. Cycads come from warm climates and so generally do not thrive outdoors in temperate areas. Most are probably best treated as summer specimens and taken into a frost-free greenhouse for the winter.

However, it is worth trying *Cycas revoluta*, the sago palm, which will survive mild winters. It is a curious plant, looking rather like a huge green shuttlecock; in the centre is a big round furry growing point which produces a complete flush of 10–20 leaves all at the same time. Plant in a sheltered location and give some extra winter protection with a screen of fleece surrounding the foliage and a little cushion of straw in the growing point. In milder winters the whole plant will survive to the next year relatively unscathed. Sometimes in a tough winter all the mature foliage will be damaged, but it is still worth keeping the plant if the growing point looks healthy. If you are lucky, the plant will flush up with a complete new set of foliage by midsummer. Do note that all parts of this plant are poisonous, and this is not the species that is used to produce the edible starch called sago.

Cycas revoluta is the most familiar of the ancient cycads and will in time make a dramatic and architectural specimen.

TENDER FOLIAGE

And now for some real celebrity foliage – the half hardy species. These are mostly fleeting summer visitors, added to an exotic garden like the icing on the cake for the final effect. Some of these exotics are green leaved but others have coloured foliage, and several also have flowers so could equally be considered in the next chapter. All are valuable, but whereas green creates a restful atmosphere, most other colours lift our spirits. In particular the warm colours such as yellow, red, orange and purple give us an instant buzz.

Coloured Leaves

Most of the tender summer foliage species are sold as bedding plants and were originally discovered by Victorian gardeners in the nineteenth century when bedding out was the fashionable garden style. Some of them are old heritage cultivars which have survived the test of time, whereas others are modern introductions and the result of complex plant-breeding programmes. Many garden designers dismiss bedding plants as bad taste, but in doing so they are ignoring a whole palette of fast-growing and vividly coloured landscape components. Exotic gardeners are leaders of fashion and don't need to worry about the shackles of conformity, so indulge yourself and plant them liberally. These are the plants

OPPOSITE PAGE: **This luscious group of summer foliage includes purple bananas underplanted with** Iresine **'Brilliantissimum',** Alternanthea **'Purple Knight' and 'Peter's Wonder' coleus.**

which add the final glittering finish to your exotic garden.

The coloured-leaved *Pelargoniums* are one group of lovely old Victorian plants that were widely used for formal bedding in the past. Many of these wonderful old favourites are still available and will make excellent additions to your exotic plantings. You should be able to obtain cultivars such as 'A Happy Thought' with pretty green and yellow butterfly leaves, 'Caroline Schmidt' with green foliage ringed with white and 'Contrast' with multicoloured leaves. All of these will also flower, but it is primarily for their vibrant foliage that you should grow them.

The curiously named beefsteak plant, *Iresine* 'Brilliantissimum' is a fast-growing plant with succulent stems and vivid bright ruby red almost translucent foliage, clearly veined in brilliant cerise. It is a striking plant, growing to about 45cm (18in). There is also a limey green form and one with narrow dark purple leaves.

Do try the sultry foliage of *Alternanthera* 'Purple Knight' or *Tradescantia* 'Purple Sabre', and contrast with the silver-leaved wire wool plant, *Calocephalus* 'Silver Sand' or the old-fashioned spider plant, *Chlorophyttum*, all of which perform well outside. The genus *Plectranthus* also has several other members which are useful, particularly the vigorous 'Silver Shield' or the spreading green and white 'Variegated Mintleaf'. The coloured-leaved versions of the sweet potato plant, *Ipomoea batatas*, also make good leafy groundcover. There is a black-leaved cultivar, not surprisingly called 'Blackie' and a limey green one called 'Marguerite', as well as a new bronze-leaved introduction worth searching out.

Helichrysum petiolare is a common but very useful neutral foliage plant for mixing in with almost

The newly introduced *Coleus* 'Henna', seen here with *Lobelia* 'Queen Victoria', has yellow leaves with a vivid red underside that glows in the sun.

Coleus – The Flame Nettles

These are fast-growing tender perennials with brilliantly coloured foliage. To be absolutely botanically correct we should now call these old Victorian favourites *Solenostemon*, but many gardeners struggle to get their tongues round this name. Their vividly coloured, jagged-edged leaves have also given them the common name of flame nettles, although they are in no way related to the stinging types. The foliage shapes vary considerably, with some fantastically fringed and curled leaves, some spotted, others ribboned with another colour or splashed with different hues in impressionist abandon.

Coleus were much loved in the mid nineteenth century and reached a height of popularity in 1868 when a collection of new cultivars was auctioned by the then penniless Royal Horticultural Society for the princely sum of £390. One single plant raised 59 guineas. The popularity of these plants coined the phrase 'coleus fever', when they were described by Shirley Hibberd in 1869 in his book. *New, Rare and Beautiful Leaved Plants.* Despite describing them in detail, he dismissed them as 'fashionable weeds'. Look for old favourites such as 'Pineapple Beauty', the novelty plant of 1877, which is still available and good over 130 years later.

Some of the old cultivars are still available and perform well. The more modern ones, such as the golden-leaved 'Pineapplette' and tomato red 'Juliet Quartermain', are excellent for planting outside as is the relatively new and intensely coloured 'Henna'. There are dozens of good cultivars, and it is worth obtaining some stock from a specialist grower, as they are then easily propagated. Do avoid the seed-raised strains which are nearly always inferior and run to flower and seed far too quickly.

If you want to feature coleus, plant them in good-sized blocks and add some vertical accent plants such as purple fountain grass or *Lobelia* 'Elmfeuer' for contrast. Coleus need a warm sheltered, well-drained site in full sun, and then they will produce a tapestry of colour often rivalling any display of flowers.

anything else. The species is an energetic, scrambling plant, with wiry stems and small hairy silver leaves the size of a thumbnail. Planted underneath larger plants such as cannas or amongst other foliage such as coleus it will ramble through and provide an excellent foil or contrast. Be warned that it is vigorous, and you will not need many plants to provide an effect. When planted in baskets or containers, it can easily behave like a baby cuckoo and take over, smothering weaker subjects. 'Limelight' is a valuable golden version of this, which borders on lime green when young. However, a word of caution – too much coloured foliage can lead to a very discordant effect, so use all these species with discretion and contrast with lots of green.

The Aroids

These lush leafy exotics all belong to the *Araceae* family and are not particularly familiar, so add an air of the unusual to our exotic garden. Most are tender and need to spend at least part of the year under frost-free greenhouse conditions, but a few are totally hardy. In general they grow to no more than waist height and so will provide some of the lower level infill in our exotic schemes. Amongst the aroids are some really handsome plants, as well as some curios and some that are quite monstrous. Most aroids are good foliage plants, but the flowers are often insignificant, unusual or just plain ugly.

Elephant's Ears

The *Colocasias*, which are sometimes called elephant's ears (not to be confused with *Bergenia,* which is also called by the same common name) are tuberous perennials producing big heart-shaped leaves on top of slender stems. *Colocasia esculenta* is commercially grown for food in warm climates (and may be called taro or eddo). Roots of this can sometimes be found in specialist food shops, and if still viable can be started into growth for the exotic garden.

There are also various ornamental types such as *C. e.* 'Fontanesii' which has broad green leaves and black stems. The notoriously difficult 'Black Magic' produces sensational matt black leaves which can grow to an immense size, so it's well worth the challenge. It needs a warm sunny location and a well-drained but rich moist soil to grow well. Grow it next to something with strong colours, such as the multi-coloured *Canna* 'Durban', and maybe underplant with a vivid red coleus such as 'Juliet Quartermain'.

To add to the confusion of common names, the similar *Alocasia* is also sometimes called elephant's ears. (I rest my case for the use of botanical names!)

Although muted in colour, *Colocasia esculenta* provides sumptuous green foliage contrasting with the spiky *Astelia nervosa* 'Westland'.

These are also leafy rhizomatous perennials, generally distinguished from *Colocasia* by the leaves which although similar are usually held vertically rather than trailing down. They are generally more difficult to grow than *Colocasia*, needing more warmth, but it is well worth trying some under glass and bringing them outdoors for display. *Alocasia* 'Portadora' and *A.* 'Calidora' both produce lush foliage under cooler conditions. As well as these there are a number of other foliage aroids which are often thought of as houseplants, such as *Dieffenbachia, Monstera* (the Swiss cheese plant) and the brilliantly coloured *Caladium,* which is notoriously tender and requires a very warm sheltered spot.

Aroids occasionally hit the news when a titan lily flowers. *Amorphophallus titanum* is probably the world's biggest and worst-smelling flower and blooms only a few times in its forty-year life span. Its foul smelling, deep purple flower can be up to 3m (10ft) across and almost as tall. Because it's a native of the Borneo rain forest, it is rarely seen except in botanic gardens, where its rare blooming always causes a sensation.

Tender Grasses

Do try the beautiful purple fountain grass, *Pennisetum setaceum* 'Rubrum', which is readily available in early summer. It is not frost hardy so has to be considered as a summer resident only, but is nevertheless well worth the extra effort. It has arching, rich purple foliage, topped in late summer by smoky pink flower heads. Use it amongst low groundcover for contrast and height. For the exotic gardener, it's a 'must have' plant.

Arundo donax 'Variegata', sometimes known as the giant reed, is an aristocrat amongst grasses, sometimes mistaken for a bamboo. This makes a huge towering plant with chunky vertical stems, draped with a waterfall of variegated arching leaves. Unfortunately it is only hardy in very mild locations. If it is damaged in a tough winter, you can cut down withered stems and it will usually re-grow again from the base. Careful gardeners will take a few plants under cover each winter as an insurance against losses.

The seed trade has recently developed a number of purple-leaved cultivars of millet, the most common of which is 'Purple Majesty'. It has rich, almost black foliage and is stiff and upright, eventually being topped by a dark brooding flowering spike. The

The waterfall foliage of *Arundo donax* 'Variegata', the giant reed grass, together with a spiky *Yucca rostrata*, and *Tetrapanax papyrifer* behind.

The broad palmate leaves of *Ricinus* 'New Zealand Purple', alongside the delicate filigree of *Sambucus* 'Black Lace' and the knobbly seedheads of *Canna indica*.

variegated form of corn, *Zea mays* 'Variegata', was a very popular plant in Victorian displays but has rather slipped from popularity and should be more widely grown. It is a vigorous annual grass, making bold vertical clumps with wide strap leaves, beautifully striped in green, white and sometimes pink. Both are annuals so must be grown from seed each year.

A purple-leaved form of sugar cane has recently been introduced. It is botanically named as *Saccharum officinarum* var. *violaceum* but is sometimes called 'Pele's Smoke'. This makes a vigorous 1.8m (6ft) clump of narrow smoky-purple foliage, a good contrast to other variegated grasses. It is borderline hardy and may well survive mild winters in sheltered locations.

The Big Boys

These next few are all tall plants that will add height to your display. Abutilons all make tall shapely spires of vine-like foliage with jolly bell-shaped flowers in many colours. 'Canary Bird' is a first-rate yellow and 'Ashford Red' a clear tomato colour, both with green foliage. The most familiar is 'Thompsonii', with yellow spotty foliage and orange flowers. Although colourful, it is coarse and gives abutilons a bad name. There are other superior variegated cultivars such as 'Cannington Peter' or 'Souvenir de Bonne'. Most will grow to around 1.5m (5ft) in a season and are best appreciated as taller plants, when the flowers are at or above eye level.

Many houseplants will be quite happy outside for the summer, either planted out or left in their pots, like these bromeliads in Will Giles's garden.

Sparrmannia africana not surprisingly comes from South Africa and makes a big imposing plant, bearing broad, slightly hairy, green leaves the size of dinner plates. Flowers are white but sparsely produced and only towards the end of the season. Position it amongst low growing plants, like colourful coleus, where it can exhibit its height and big green leaves.

The castor oil plants, members of the genus *Ricinus*, are fast-growing annuals. The most attractive are those with bronze foliage such as the cultivar 'Carmencita Bright Red'. Seed is readily available and quickly produces a plant with huge palmate leaves in glossy bronze. In late summer, small flowers are formed, followed by attractive reddish prickly seedpods, not unlike colourful conkers. It is worth

searching for a new cultivar called 'New Zealand Purple', which produces a strapping plant with deep purple, highly polished leaves. Like all purple foliage, you can mix it effectively with almost all other colours. Don't forget that all *Ricinus* are highly poisonous, so should be handled with care and not planted in gardens with children.

Houseplants on Holiday

To add a real touch of the tropical to an exotic display, there is no reason why you cannot give your houseplants a vacation and plant them outside for the summer. Many of these will grow outdoors quite happily, providing they are kept moist and not allowed to burn in the full sun. The Victorians bedded out all sorts of exotica quite successfully, so it's well worth while experimenting with a selection of plants from your favourite nursery or the houseplant section at the supermarket. Various types of rubber plants, aspidistra, *Tradescantia*, *Monstera*, shrimp plants, *Sansevieria* and *Dracaena* are all likely to be quite successful. Don't be restricted by this list; select what appeals to you and give it a try. After all, many of these plants are regularly used for display in stuffy offices and draughty entrances and abused in shopping malls, so they are certainly tolerant plants.

You may also like to try bromeliads, sometimes called urn plants, because of the funnel shaped leaf structure. These would naturally grow in the cracks of trees in a rainforest and are correctly known as epiphytes. You can try to imitate this in the garden by tying them on to suitable trees, with a ball of moss around the roots. Alternatively they look attractive either displayed in pots or planted in small shady corners. There are many different types, some with very brightly coloured foliage, such as the variegated form of the fruiting pineapple, *Ananas comosus* 'Variegatus'. Spanish moss, *Tillandsia usneoides,* is another epiphyte. You will recognize it as the greyish wispy foliage that drips from trees in warmer climates. If you can find it, simply hang it on a suitable branch and occasionally dampen to keep it alive.

Gingers

These are fast-growing, rhizomatous perennials with lush foliage and the bonus of late summer flowers so could quite logically be in the next chapter. The spice ginger actually comes from one species, which is not a good garden plant. Most of the ornamentals are members of the genus *Hedychium*. They make substantial clumps of lush green foliage, topped in late summer by spectacular, sweet scented spidery flowers in white, yellow, pink and orange. Of the many available, *Hedychium gardnerianum* with lemon yellow flowers and red stamens and *H. coccineum* 'Tara' with tight spikes of scented orange flowers are both reliable, but there are many others to try.

As well as the *Hedychiums* there are other related gingers such as *Cautleya spicata*, a very tough hardy ginger from the Himalayas with green foliage and ruby flowering stems topped with red bracts and lemon yellow flowers. It looks good in a shady location under tree ferns. *Curcuma* species have only recently become popular but are often available now as flowering plants in late summer with curious magnolia-like pink flowers. The clumsily named *Alpinia zerumbet* 'Variegata' is a tender species grown mainly for its boldly variegated yellow and green foliage. Contrast it with dark foliage such as *Alternanthera* 'Purple Knight'. Start them under glass and move outside for summer display.

The edible ginger is produced from *Zingiber officinale,* which is a tropical plant and really not suitable for growing in temperate gardens, even in summer. It's also not particularly attractive but can be grown in a heated greenhouse for its curiosity value!

Hedychium gardnerianum, one of the ginger lilies from the Himalayas, has exotic sweet-scented flowers as well as lush green foliage.

EXOTIC FLOWERS

Whilst nearly all natural rainforests will be predominantly green, most of you who dabble with exotic gardening will want to add the 'razzle dazzle' that colourful flowers provide. Flowers in an exotic garden need to be bright, flamboyant, preferably large and ideally a little bit unusual. After all, you don't want your exotic garden to look like a traditional English herbaceous border or a cottage garden. There are no rules as to what you can use or not use and the choice will be yours, but try to think Picasso and Monet rather than Gainsborough.

Dahlias

Most people either love or loathe dahlias. They are certainly in-your-face plants, with big blowsy blooms in the loudest of colours, but it is because of these characteristics that they're just ideal plants for the exotic garden. The late Christopher Lloyd loved them and used them throughout his exotic garden at Great Dixter. Dahlias originate from Mexico and are tender plants that grow from fleshy tubers. They will not tolerate any frost so cannot be planted out until summer has well and truly arrived. Over the years they have been highly hybridized, and there are thousands of cultivars available.

The National Collection of Dahlias is held in the UK by Winchester Growers with a staggering 1,700 cultivars. They are also commercial bulb and flower producers and in recent years, have been introducing

OPPOSITE PAGE: *Dahlia* **'Bishop of Llandaff' was raised nearly ninety years ago but is still a very effective plant, seen here in front of** *Abutilon* **'Savitzei'.**

many new cultivars and in particular stunning single-flowered dahlias with dark foliage. 'Twyning's Revel' has soft pink flowers and 'Perfect Partner' has white blooms, both with dark leaves. Their recent exhibits at the Chelsea Flower Show have received well-deserved Gold Medals.

The dark-leaved cultivars are very effective, both for their blossoms and also their foliage. The best known of these is the 'Bishop of Llandaff', which has finely cut bronze foliage and single scarlet flowers with a yellow centre. It was raised in the 1920s and is still a good garden plant. Plant it with the red-leaved coleus 'Juliet Quartermain' and the white variegated *Abutilon* 'Savizei'. 'David Howard' is a fully double orange cultivar which has bronze foliage. Both grow to about 90cm (3ft). *Dahlia* 'Moonfire' is another reliable but shorter dark-leaved cultivar, which produces a multitude of single orange flowers flushed with red. Try it with purple fountain grass and the silver leaves of *Centaurea gymnocarpa*. All of these are excellent providers of exotic colour, with their vivid flowers set against muted bronze foliage.

There is no shortage of other good dahlias, such as 'Berger's Rekord', a good clear red; 'Orfeo', a fine rich purple; or 'Arabian Night', which is a deep ruby colour, almost dark enough to be called black.

Dahlia imperialis is sometimes called the tree dahlia, as it will make as much as 2m (7ft) of luxuriant foliage in a season. Do start it early and feed generously, as it looks at its best when it is tall enough for you to see the undersides of the leaves, which are a delicate almost iridescent purple. It sometimes flowers with a small insignificant pale pink flower but very late in the season, and you are unlikely to see this unless you have a very sheltered spot and warm late autumn. Enjoy it as a small leafy exotic 'tree'.

Cannas

Cannas are as flamboyant as a row of Vegas showgirls. They are bright, colourful and thoroughly entertaining. There's nothing really sophisticated about them at all – they are sheer and absolute fun. Not only do they have large, lush leaves but huge, gaudy flowers, repeatedly produced over many weeks. In a single season they will grow to the height of a man and seldom fail to perform as they should. If you were to take a time machine back to the mid-nineteenth century, you would find that cannas featured highly in the fashionable gardens of the time. They were very much *de rigeur* in the gardening world, reported in the gardening press and highly hybridized by the plant breeders of the time. Such accolades are still relevant today, as they are excellent garden plants.

You can get cannas in any height from dwarfs, growing not much more than 45cm (18in) up to lush giants of 2m (7ft). There are no blue cannas, and white is the holy grail of canna breeders, although most so-called whites are pale primrose yellows. Flower colour goes through most of the spectrum, from pale primrose yellow, shades of orange to rich reds and various shades of pink. Most colours are available with either green or bronze foliage. Some cultivars exhibit leaves with more complex confections of gold, pink, purple or white. They usually start flowering in mid-summer and will go on until the first frosts in the autumn.

Cannas are tropical plants that originated in South America and the West Indies. One of the basic species, *Canna indica* was first imported to the UK in 1596 but it wasn't until the nineteenth century that cannas developed from leggy plants with small flowers to more compact plants with large flowers. Over the second half of the nineteenth century and the early twentieth century they were exceedingly popular both in Europe and America, and many new hybrids were produced. However fashions changed and cannas slipped from popularity for the majority of the twentieth century until the 1990s, when they once again started to gain popularity.

The cannas in this exotic border are planted in groups in a formal Victorian style and surrounded by coloured-leaved pelargoniums and spiky leaved *Chlorophytum*.

There are hundreds of different cultivars, and it is difficult to know which ones to suggest. If you are able to visit a specialist nursery, you may find some really exquisite cultivars available in small quantities, and these can provide beautiful accents in our exotic garden. However for general use, there are a few really good reliable cultivars which are readily available. Probably the best-known is the tall orange cultivar with bronze leaves called 'Wyoming'; it's a real reliable toughie that performs well every time. Its counterpart with red flowers is called 'Assaut' – very similar to 'King Humbert'. There is a good clear yellow with green leaves called 'Richard Wallace', and various yellows with red spots such as 'En Avant'. The best pink is a tall cultivar called *Canna iridiflora* 'Ehemannii', which has lush green leaves and long sprays of somewhat trailing flowers. You might also look out for the distinctive *Canna* 'Panache', which produces a more delicate spidery flowerhead in a pale apricot, flushed deep pink. Although less brash than many of the others, it is still bold enough to include in the exotic garden.

'Cleopatra' is a fun cultivar and worth growing for its curiosity value. It is basically a green-leaved *Canna* which sometimes produces shoots with attractive bronze stripes on its leaves or even totally bronze shoots. Alongside this, whilst all the green shoots

The vibrant blooms of *Canna* 'Wyoming' seen through the filigree of lavender provided by *Verbena bonariense*.

produce yellow flowers with faint red spots, there are often flower variations with red splashes in the petals. Any totally bronze shoots will produce handsome tomato red flowers. Technically this schizophrenic plant is a mutation, but it's fun to grow. If you buy 'Cleopatra', choose a plant that is already showing some variation in the young growth.

Although many gardeners grow cannas for their flowers, we must also highlight the foliage cannas. The most startling of all is 'Durban', sometimes also sold as 'Phasion' or incorrectly as 'Tropicanna'. This has psychedelic purple foliage, vividly striped with pink, which fades to cream, together with rich orange flowers. It is undoubtedly the most outrageous of all cannas. The similar 'Striata' (syn 'Pretoria') has green leaves, striped with yellow plus orange flowers. For sumptuous green foliage, use the tall-growing *Canna musifolia* or its big brother 'Grande', neither of which tend to flower. *Canna indica* 'Purpurea' is a good bronze foliage plant with the added bonus of masses of small orange flowers. Both make huge specimens in a single season.

All cannas look best in generous groups, so locate good chunky plants in drifts of threes, fives or more. As most cannas are tall, they associate well with shorter plants, and it helps to plant something low growing around their 'legs'. Using silver foliage such as *Helichrysum petiolare* or *Centaurea gymnocarpa* around the bronze-leaved types is particularly successful.

Both the foliage and flowers of *Canna* 'Cleopatra' are unstable and produce considerable variations which, although not beautiful, are fascinating.

More Blowsy Blooms

There are of course lots of other flowers suitable for the exotic garden, including tall plants providing much-needed height as well as exotic climbers.

Begonias, with their many different types and season-long colour are just the plants for an exotic border. The 'Non Stops' produce big showy double flowers in a huge range of colours, some with bronze foliage. The cultivar 'Pin-Up Flame' has huge saucer-sized single flowers, almost like giant frilly pansies, in a rich shade of orange tinted red. 'Dragon Wing Red' is a small red-flowered begonia but one which produces masses of blooms. It has wonderfully glossy green foliage and an upright habit which arches with the weight of flowers as it matures. Begonias are all very tolerant, growing equally well in both sun and shade, provided they are kept reasonably moist, and flowering from June through to the frosts. Use as colourful groundcover or in containers.

Petunias are so familiar but very colourful and reliable for hot sunny spots. Try the newer 'Wave' types for a sheet of colour, or the large-flowered 'Surfinias'. If you opt for seed-raised types, choose a good F1 hybrid strain such as 'Frenzy', which is available in a multitude of colours and has good rain resistance.

Busy Lizzies, correctly known as *Impatiens* used to be simple windowsill plants, but the plant breeders' efforts in recent years have resulted in a huge range of brilliantly coloured plants. Probably some of the best for the exotic garden are the New Guinea Impatiens, which produce large flowers over a long period of time, some with variegated foliage. The recent 'Fusion' range has shell-shaped flowers, including some unusual yellow and orange shades. A curious species, called *Impatiens niamniamensis* 'Congo

The brilliant red flower spikes and bronze leaves of *Lobelia* 'Elmfeuer' contrasted by the colourful foliage of *Coleus* 'Henna' and *Pelargonium* 'Contrast'.

Cockatoo' is an upright Busy Lizzie, with unusual shaped yellow and red flowers, with a very dominant spur filled with nectar. There is a variegated version – doubly attractive.

Most people think of *Lobelia* as the diminutive blue edging plant so often twinned with sickly white alyssum. However there are also some excellent tall types with brilliant flowers, some with bronze foliage. The cultivar 'Queen Victoria' has been around quite a while and produces gleaming scarlet spikes on top of spires of glossy bronze foliage. It is a hardy herbaceous perennial but is tediously prone to wilt when dry. If you water, it will recover, but the flower spikes remain annoyingly kinked. So plant in a damp situation or keep well watered. The newer cultivar 'Elmfeuer' is worth looking out for and is a great improvement on the old 'Queen Victoria'. It looks spectacular with Coleus 'Henna'.

Fuchsias are generally a little too twee to compete with other exotics, but there are a few worth trying. *Fuchsia boliviana* comes from South America and makes a large bush, eventually sporting huge trusses of long fluorescent red tapering trumpets. It has curious peeling bark rather like a small birch tree. It is worth including as a curiosity in a quiet corner of our exotic garden. *Fuchsia* 'Thalia' is one of a group of Triphylla fuchsias, characterized by leaves in groups of three and flowers in terminal clusters. The foliage is a muted bronze, tinted purple – a good foil for the rich orange tubular flowers. Plant with the yellow *Canna* 'Richard Wallace' and limey foliage of *Helichryssum* 'Limelight'.

The Cape fuchsias from South Africa are members of the genus *Phygelius,* and despite some similarity they are not related to fuchsias. These are potentially useful plants in the exotic garden but can be disappointing. So try a few Cape fuchsias and see how they perform for you, but don't base your whole display on them. The older cultivar 'Winchester Fanfare' produces tall arching stems with red flowers and tiny lemon yellow centres. It's best viewed from below, so plant at the top of a bank or in a raised bed. There are some good yellows such as 'Yellow Trumpet' and 'Moonraker', an excellent cerise pink called 'Sensation', and a golden-leaved cultivar called 'Sunshine'. Some are inclined to run and can be invasive, so plant with care in a warm sunny location.

Lofty Flowers

Contrasting heights in any display always adds extra interest. The tall *Brugmansias* with their big, bright and blowsy flowers are real head-turners. Their huge, brilliantly coloured trumpets in white, pinks and yellows are perfect constituents of our exotic garden. Ideally keep them from year to year, so you get

Solanum rantonettii makes a tall plant with vivid blue flowers, and the variegated form displayed here also has attractive foliage.

specimens with flowers above eye level. Nearly all have a rich perfume, and some have variegated foliage.

Although blue is not one of my preferred colours for the exotic garden, *Plumbago capensis* with its masses of small pale blue flowers is one of those plants which is seen in so many warm climates and seems to just shout exotic. However it does not flower readily on a small plant, so it is worth growing a sizeable plant in a pot or a large tub and keeping it from year to year. Although you can plant it out, it is possibly one of those plants that is best kept as a container plant. It is a loose wiry shrub and so can be allowed to grow freely in the summer months and then cut back hard before returning to the greenhouse in the autumn.

Amongst the annual climbers, *Ipomoea lobata* is one of the most colourful and is easily grown from seed sown in the spring.

Solanum rantonnetii also makes a tall lax plant with blue flowers.

One classic exotic we must discuss is *Bougainvillea*, another plant which is endemic throughout the landscapes in warmer climates, producing clouds of brilliantly coloured bracts. Sadly this plant is difficult to grow in a temperate exotic garden. It must be over-wintered under glass and needs to be pruned carefully to make sure you retain the flowering wood. They take up a great deal of space in a greenhouse over winter, have vicious spines and really don't thrive in our watery temperate sunshine. Having said that, there are a couple of specimens outside an Italian restaurant in London which seem to survive and even flower despite neglect and a cruel pruning regime. However in general, better to enjoy them on holidays abroad.

Ramblers and Scramblers

Amongst the seasonal plants, there are also a few colourful and fast-growing climbers that are appealing and unusual enough to add to an exotic border. One of the most attractive is *Ipomoea lobata* (syn *Mina lobata*) which has delicate spikes of small flowers that graduate from red buds through to a warm cream when fully open. The overall two-tone effect is very fetching. Plant it to scramble through bronze-leaved cannas such as 'Wyoming'. The genus *Ipomoea* also includes the morning glories, and these are also fast growing climbers, producing vivid trumpets in red, blue or white. Although each individual flower lasts only a day, they are replaced continuously throughout the summer.

Thunbergia alata, familiarly known as Black Eyed Susan, is another colourful annual climber, producing brilliant orange flowers with black centres. In recent years, new versions have appeared such as 'Susie Mixed', which as well as orange flowers includes pale yellow and white, some with the typical black centre and some with clear centres. Also look out for the 'African Sunset' mixture, which includes some lovely dark, rich colours as well as some two-tone flowers. It also looks spectacular in a hanging basket as it both trails and climbs up the chains.

The double form of the tiger lily, *Lilium lancifolium* 'Flore Plena', contrasted against bold banana foliage and the silvery fans of a blue Mexican palm.

The rarely grown *Rhodochiton atrosanguineus* is a light-weight climber with deep purple flowers surrounded by a bright pink calyx, rather like an elongated fuchsia. It flowers in the first year from seed but it is actually perennial so can be left in place for future years. Finally you may like to try *Cobaea scandens*, the cup and saucer vine, which has large cup-shaped flowers set against a dominant, saucer-like calyx. This climber is commonly available in a deep velvety purple, although there is also a very attractive greenish white form 'Alba' that is worth searching out. You can plant these climbers to scramble up over evergreen shrubs or through some of the more tender summer foliage plants such as *Grevillea robusta* or *Sparmannia africana*. Remember though that any of these climbers will need a fair start,

without too much competition, so plant in good soil in an open location and then when they are growing vigorously, tie the shoots to a cane and lead them into the plant you want them to scramble through.

Exotic Bulbs

There are many bulbs, corms and tubers that come from warm Mediterranean areas that will make welcome flourishes in our exotic garden. As many will be tender, probably the easiest way to grow them is in pots, starting them in a cool greenhouse. Plant several bulbs in a 12cm (5in) pot and then move outside in early summer, when growth has started but before

As well as strikingly beautiful flowers, *Brugmansias* produce a sweet perfume that is strongest at night.

they become lush and flop. Growing them in this way also gives you a supply of filler plants that can be used to plug a gap in your border.

Lilies are a huge group of plants containing a myriad of different varieties in all sorts of colours, with countless bright yellows, oranges, brick reds and rich pinks that can be used in the exotic garden. Older cultivars such as 'Connecticut King', 'Enchantment' and *Lilium regale* are reliable performers.

There are many other bulbs. The pineapple lilies, different types of *Eucomis*, are somewhat refined looking with pale pink or greenish ivory flowers. They can be planted permanently and mulched each winter or grown in pots. *Crocosmias* grow from corms and have bright green sword-like foliage and brilliant orange or red flowers. *Alstroemerias* grow from small tubers, and many of the modern cultivars flower for an extended period of time. They are mostly available as partly grown plants in the spring. Avoid the very short cultivars, which tend to lack presence. Check out the catalogues for other summer bulbs such as *Sparaxis, Tigridia, Ixia* and *Watsonia* that are readily available in the spring and are worth exploring.

In recent years a number of brilliantly coloured hybrid *Zantedeschia* have appeared on the market, often sold as calla lilies (although they are neither lilies nor members of the genus *Calla*) in various shades of smoky pink, vibrant orange, glowing yellow and even a rich purplish black. Although tricky to grow and expensive, the flowers do last for a long time. Buy them ready grown rather than as dry bulbs and use as infill plants for extra summer colour.

Gladioli

Traditional gladioli have become unfashionable but their bold, bright spikes of huge flowers are ideal for the exotic garden. The Victorians used to plant some amongst cannas, and the similar-looking flowers masqueraded as early canna blooms. As gladioli need to be planted earlier than most summer exotics, it pays to start them in pots. Plant about five bulbs in a 12.5cm (5in) pot in mid spring and keep cool and moist; outdoors is fine. By the time you are planting your tender exotics in early summer, the gladioli will be partly grown and can be mixed in with other plants. Choose some of the big bold cultivars with red, orange or purple flowers to contrast with your other exotics. 'Purple Flora' is a striking rich violet colour and 'Princess Margaret Rose' is a vibrant orange. Don't be afraid of clashing colours. Gladioli only flower for a short period of time and so a sudden burst of shocking colour can be quite exhilarating.

Fragrant Exotics

Visiting an exotic garden should be an event where all the senses are assaulted by powerful experiences. If we are trying to imitate a jungle, possibly the real smell of an exotic garden should be a damp musty smell, maybe more rotting vegetation than Chanel. However considering the sensitivities of our visitors, we should probably aim for something more sanitized.

Sadly there are relatively few exotic plants which have scent. The gingers (*Hedychium spp*) are the first to come to mind, which have exotic foliage, flowers and a rich perfume, and of course angel's trumpets *(Brugmansia spp)* with their richly scented flowers. Amongst the permanent hardier planting, the pittosporums will give us a delicious chocolate smell and *Euphorbia mellifera* a hint of honey. The old-fashioned heliotrope or cherry pie is a very richly scented tender perennial, but you must select the older named cultivars such as 'Princess Marina', 'Chatsworth' or 'White Lady'. Modern cultivars sadly have little scent. The seed-raised tobacco plants include a wonderful tall one called *Nicotiana sylvestris,* which has been rebranded by the nursery trade as 'Only the Lonely'. It produces stately spikes of white flowers, like November 5th rockets, complete with a sweet perfume. Another huge group of plants, many of which have rich perfume, are the lilies, perfect late additions to the exotic garden.

When positioning scented plants do remember to locate them where the scent can be best appreciated. For example position angel's trumpets next to a footpath, and possibly some heliotrope alongside a seat. There are also of course aromatic plants that we can touch, such as the peppermint scented *Pelargonium tomentosum,* and these will also need to be planted where you can gently rub your fingers across the foliage.

PROPAGATING EXOTICS

Many gardeners find that propagating plants is one of the most exciting aspects of horticulture. Seeing cuttings root and seedlings grow, eventually maturing to full size plants, gives a great sense of achievement. Although it's possible to create a beautiful exotic garden without propagating any of your own plants, it is likely to be a lot more costly and probably less satisfying. Although many of the plants you will want to use are readily available, there are also many other less familiar species which you can try, if you have the facilities and patience, to propagate and grow your own. Dashing down to your garden early on a summer's morning to see if your new home-grown treasure has opened its flowers is a magical experience.

Greenhouses

In order to propagate plants for the exotic garden, you really need a greenhouse, although a good well-constructed polythene tunnel may also be useful. Greenhouses are relatively inexpensive and much more useful and substantial than polytunnels.

For exotics, you need as large a greenhouse as you can afford and fit into your garden. Inevitably you will end up wanting to grow more each year, and tender plants have the disconcerting habit of getting bigger each year. The smallest viable size is 2m × 2.5m (6ft × 8ft). Buy one that is tall enough to overwinter

OPPOSITE PAGE: **Batches of colourful *Iresine* and the feathery *Cyperus* growing on in a small greenhouse ready for planting out in summer.**

big specimen plants and with a door wide enough to take a wheelbarrow laden with heavy plants. A good greenhouse should have adequate ventilation, at both high and low levels, ideally equipped with autovent openers – simple devices that will open the vents automatically on a warm day, well worth the extra cost. Position your greenhouse in an open, sunny spot but ideally with shelter from wind.

Heating a Greenhouse

To really dabble in exotic propagation, you will need some heating. If you are going to attempt to keep tender plants over winter you will also need to be able to keep the greenhouse at least frost-free and ideally warmer. And besides the obvious benefits there is something very exciting about escaping into a heated greenhouse, full of exotic plants, in mid winter.

Electric greenhouse heaters are possible and have the advantage of thermostatic control, but they will be the most expensive to run. Paraffin heaters are cheap, but they have little control and must be refuelled frequently. Heaters run from bottled gas are an excellent option and will have some thermostatic control. You can even get a changeover valve which operates with two bottles of gas, so that when one runs out, the supply transfers to the second. This is most important to avoid the gas failing on a frosty night.

You can reduce heating bills and help to maintain a more even temperature by lining a greenhouse with bubble wrap in winter. Stretching polythene or bubble wrap across the greenhouse just above head height also reduces heating bills. You can even restrict the heated area with a temporary partition made from

These abutilons were rooted as autumn cuttings and have been slowly grown on over winter, with the stems tied to a cane and the sideshoots trimmed.

polythene to create a smaller warmer zone. Don't forget though that this will have the disadvantage of reducing valuable winter light, so plants may become leggier. Remove such extra insulation as soon as the worst of the winter is past and consider additional lighting.

Equipment

For growing exotics, you will need some bench space and some floor space for taller plants. Plants such as *Abutilons*, bananas and *Brugmansias* can be grown on the floor, without touching the glass. Benching is equally useful, as it brings smaller plants closer to working height, making watering and tending them much easier. Plants requiring low light can also be grown under the bench. Cannas and gingers also overwinter well under a bench, where the light drip of water will keep them from desiccating.

For exotics, you will need a heated propagating area. Seeds require base heat, and cuttings require heat plus an enclosed environment. Invest in a small electric propagator complete with a heating element, and it will serve you for years. Most seeds and cuttings need a temperature of around 21°C (70°F) to germinate or root, and it is much more efficient to heat a propagator to this temperature than a whole greenhouse. For those that do not have electricity in the greenhouse, it will be simpler to site such a propagator on a windowsill in the house and then transfer seedlings and rooted cuttings to the greenhouse when established.

Composts

All propagation and plant production requires the use of special growing media – often called potting composts. (Do not use garden soil in containers in a greenhouse.) Seed composts have very low nutrient levels and are used for seed sowing. Potting composts will have more nutrients and are used for pricking out and potting young plants. A compost for cuttings can easily be made by mixing equal parts of sharp sand and peat, or peat and fine bark. There are also many proprietary multi-purpose composts available which do not perform perfectly for any one function but will be adequate for most purposes and avoid the need for lots of different bags.

Traditionally most potting composts were made from a mix of loam (soil), peat and sand. A range of standard mixes was developed called the John Innes Composts, and these are still available and very good for some uses. There is a John Innes Seed Compost, then three potting composts with increasing levels of nutrition. For short, they are often labelled JIP1, JIP2 and JIP3. The latter is still good for large pots containing permanent plants such as palms.

Modern composts are often called loamless composts. They are usually based on peat, sometimes mixed with other materials together with a balance of fertilizers and are suitable for exotics. In recent years there has also been a move away from peat-based composts for environmental reasons, and now non-peat or peat-reduced composts are available, based on materials such as coir, bark, wood chips or other recycled materials. Although these can produce acceptable results they are nowhere near as easy to use, and the results can be disappointing. Peat-based composts generally remain the most popular, predictable and effective.

Propagation Techniques

Although there are a myriad of plants you may grow in your exotic garden, propagation techniques are actually quite basic, and many familiar plants can be propagated by seed, cuttings or division with a few variations. Providing you follow the basic principles, a high degree of success is likely and you will find the results of propagating your own plants very rewarding.

Growing from Seed

Seed is the commonest means by which plants reproduce and spread themselves in nature. Over the twentieth century, vast changes were made in the quality of plants available from seed, and there are many excellent types suitable for your exotic garden. Plants designated as F1 hybrids will be likely to give particularly good performance and be worth the extra cost of the seed.

Sowing seeds of exotics follows all the basic traditional principles. Seeds require three basics for germination – water, warmth and air. Small seeds such as Marigolds, *Nicotiana* or *Rudbeckia* are best sown in bulk in a seed tray and pricked out into trays or individual pots. Larger seeds such as *Ricinus,* banana, *Canna* or *Zea* can be sown individually in small 75mm (3in) pots, dibbling two seeds in each pot. If both grow you can remove the weaker. Very hard seeds

---

EXOTICS FROM SEED

Alternanthera 'Purple Knight'
Begonia – 'Non Stop' strains and 'Dragon Wing Red'
Celosia plumosa cultivars
Cobaea scandens
French and African Marigolds
Impatiens cultivars
Ipomoea lobata
Millet 'Purple Majesty'
Nicotiana 'Only the Lonely'
Petunia 'Frenzy Strains'
Ricinus cultivars
Rudbeckia 'Prairie Sun'
Thunbergia alata
Zea mays 'Variegata'

---

such as canna or banana must have the seed coat nicked gently using a small file or hacksaw blade to just break through to the pale inner tissues. The seed is then soaked in warm water for 48 hours before sowing individually in small pots or cells.

Normally you should finish off the sowing process by covering with a sheet of black polythene, to keep out the light and help retain the moisture. Some seeds may require light and so should not be covered, although the packet will usually remind you of this. Don't forget to finish off all sown seeds with a clearly written label. Most seeds of tender exotic plants will require a temperature of around 21°C (70°F).

Check sown seeds daily, water as necessary and turn the polythene to prevent undue accumulation of condensation. As soon as there is any sign of germination, the black plastic should be removed. For the first day or so seedlings should be kept in light shade to avoid scorching, then move to full light to ensure that they grow into sturdy seedlings.

Seeds sown in bulk will need to be pricked out into further trays of 35 or 48 seedlings or individually to small pots, usually 9cm (3½in) or cell trays. Seeds sown in individual pots will not need pricking out.

TOP LEFT: **Sowing seeds using a pinching action.**

BOTTOM LEFT: **Covering seeds with sieved compost.**

BELOW: **Pricking out young seedlings into trays.**

Water in the seedlings lightly and grow on in a warm, light environment.

Cuttings

Many tender exotics can be easily propagated by taking cuttings. Always use a sharp knife for preparing cuttings. There are two main seasons when we take cuttings of exotics: late summer or early spring.

In late summer or early autumn, you will need to take cuttings of all plants that you want to keep for next year before they are damaged by frosts. In particular there will be those such as *Abutilons, Sparmannia* and *Brugmansia* that need a long growing season to produce good-sized specimens before next summer. Autumn cuttings are sometimes called semi-ripe, as the shoots have become firm.

Most of the smaller filler plants such as *Coleus, Iresine, Tradescantia* and *Helichrysum* can be propagated by spring cuttings, and because of their speed of growth they will make good plants by early summer. Spring cuttings may also be called softwood cuttings. In order to have stock for spring cuttings, you will either have to lift stock plants from your beds and overwinter them, or root just a few cuttings in the

autumn to provide parent plants for the main batch of cuttings in the spring. Most grow very fast, and an autumn rooted *Helichrysum* or coleus for example, if grown on and pinched, will yield twenty or more cuttings the following spring.

Tip cuttings are the simplest and are used for propagating many tender exotic plants such as *Coleus, Iresine* or *Pelargoniums*. These are prepared by removing the soft tip of a shoot when it is actively growing. It is reduced to about 7cm (3in) with about three leaves or pairs of leaves. The base of the cutting is trimmed just below a node. Some of the lower leaves should be removed to leave a bare stem.

Most cuttings root easily, but if you are doubtful, or if the species is known to be difficult, dip the cuttings into hormone rooting powder before inserting into pots of rooting compost. Several cuttings can usually be inserted around the edge of a pot. For larger quantities, seed trays, cell trays or peat pellets can be used. Cuttings have no roots and so we must ensure

BELOW RIGHT: **Rooting an individual cutting in a Jiffy 7 peat pellet.**

BELOW: **Hormone rooting powder is used for this autumn *Abutilon* cutting.**

that they remain as moist as possible by placing them in a closed propagating frame or within a plastic bag.

Any cuttings with particularly large leaves, such as *Brugmansia, Sparrmannia* and some leafy abutilons, should have the leaf area reduced to slow the loss of water by transpiration. Do this by laying the cutting on a firm base and cutting back the size of mature leaves by 50 per cent.

Dahlias can also be propagated from cuttings. In this case the stock will have been overwintered as tubers, which are swollen fleshy roots. In early spring these can be set very shallowly in seed trays of compost and kept moist and warm at around 10°C (50°F). They will very rapidly produce soft green shoots which can be used as cuttings. They should be taken whilst short and stocky and not allowed to grow

ABOVE: **Selecting a suitable shoot for a tip cutting in spring.**

BELOW: **Rooting cuttings in a closed humid propagator.**

ABOVE: **Removing lower leaves and trimming below a node.**

BELOW: **A well-rooted coleus cutting ready for potting.**

lush or the stems will become hollow and they will not root. You should be able to get several batches of cuttings from last year's tubers and in this way bulk up favourite cultivars. The stock tuber can be left to grow on and also be used for planting if needed.

Newly rooted cuttings are quite fragile. Always slowly acclimatize them to normal conditions, removing the trays or pots from the propagator but still keeping them lightly shaded and damped over for a few days. When nicely established, they can be potted up separately in potting compost in individual pots. Again keep shaded and damped over until settled in their new pots. Be especially careful to wean cuttings in spring, when conditions can sometimes be unexpectedly warm and sunny. Many plants also respond well to being pinched, a week or so after potting, to encourage sideshoots and a bushy habit.

Many plants such as these young coleus respond well to pinching, which encourages sideshoots and a well-shaped bushy plant.

AUTUMN SEMI-RIPE CUTTINGS

Abutilon – all cultivars
Brugmansia – all cultivars
Centaurea gymnocarpa
Fuchsias – all types
Lantana camara cultivars
Osteospermum cultivars
Plumbago capensis
Sparmannia africana
Streptosolon jamesonii

SPRING SOFTWOOD CUTTINGS

Bidens cultivars
Coleus – all cultivars
Dahlia – all types
Helichrysum petiolare & 'Limelight'
Iresine – all types
Pelargoniums – all types
Plectranthus – all cultivars
Tradescantia 'Purple Sabre'
Tropaelum ' Hermine Grasshof'

Division

A few of the exotics that you will be growing are herbaceous perennials and can therefore be propagated by division. A good example of this is the perennial *Lobelia* 'Queen Victoria'. Stock of this should be lifted from the border in the autumn, kept semi-dormant and just frost-free over the winter. In early spring gently pull the clump apart into smaller sections, ideally each part having three to five small shoots. Each division should be potted up into a new pot, approximately 10cm (4in) using potting compost. Water in well and grow on in an unheated greenhouse.

TOP LEFT: **Dividing a clump of lobelia by pulling the shoots apart.** RIGHT: **The new division goes into a clean 10cm (4in) pot.** BOTTOM LEFT: **Fill with good potting compost and gently firm in.**

Dividing Cannas

Cannas are also propagated by division, although the process is slightly different as they grow from swollen structures called rhizomes. Overwintered stock should be plump and not shrivelled, ideally showing prominent buds or small green shoots. Gently shake the old soil off the clump, so that you can clearly see the rhizomes and the new shoots. Sometimes you can pull the clumps apart, although you may need a sharp knife to cut through some of the rhizomes. Remember that canna virus is easily transmitted and so you should sterilize your knife with a horticultural disinfectant before moving on to another clump. Ideally each new division should contain three to five shoots.

Use 15–20cm (6–8in) pots and half fill with potting compost. You may need to put more than one division in a pot to get a good well-balanced plant. Complete filling the pots with compost to leave any new shoots just poking out of the surface of the compost. Remember that, until they flower, cannas are very difficult to identify and so put a label in each pot. Freshly divided cannas need to go into a warm greenhouse, ideally at between 50–60°F (10–16°C). Water them sparingly to start with, as they do not have any roots and so can easily rot if they are kept too wet. As soon as you start to see leaves growing vigorously, you can then water regularly and generously. Keep them in full light and well fed until ready for planting out in early summer. Gingers are treated in the same way.

Special Techniques

Although not difficult, a few plants require slightly different treatment to achieve success.

Brugmansia Cuttings

The Angel's Trumpets can be rooted from long hardwood cuttings. In early autumn, before plants are cleared from the beds, cut up stems into sections about 30–45cm (12–18in) long. These should be trimmed just above a bud at the top and just below a bud at the bottom. Remove all the mature leaves but retain the small buds and tiny sideshoots. Insert them

RIGHT: **Dividing a dormant clump of *Canna* rhizomes.**

BELOW RIGHT: **Positioning the new divisions in a clean 20cm (8in) pot.**

BELOW: **Filled with good compost, leaving young shoots showing.**

A hardwood *Brugmansia* stem cutting, prepared and ready for insertion into a pot of rooting compost.

trim to sections of about 25–30cm (9–12in), removing all the leaves. You then need either a gravel tray, which is like a seed tray without drainage holes, or an ordinary seed tray lined with polythene. This is filled with water, and the prepared cuttings are floated on the surface. The tray needs to be placed in a warm environment, ideally a propagator with bottom heating, around 21°C (70°F). Over a period of several weeks, the stems will send out roots and small shoots from the joints. Top up the water as necessary and replace if it becomes stagnant. When the new small plants look strong, you can chop up the old stem, separating the new plants, which can be potted individually into small pots of new compost. Remember that any roots produced in water are very fragile and will easily snap, so handle with great care. The new plants should be weaned carefully, keeping them moist and shaded until they are established and growing on.

Arundo donax 'Variegata' cutting prepared and being laid in a shallow container of clean water.

the right way up, with four or five cuttings around a 12cm (5in) pot of rooting compost, and gently firm them in. Keep warm and moist, but as they do not have leaves, they do not need to be in a propagator, just a warm greenhouse. They will root and grow away quite quickly and then can be potted individually to grow on over the winter. Such large cuttings will quickly make good sized plants.

Brugmansias do not flower until the stem has forked, so the quicker the plant reaches this stage, the better. Keep them growing on in a warm greenhouse at around 10°C (50°F), potting on when the roots fill the pots.

Arundo donax 'Variegata'

This exotic grass is expensive to buy but can be easily propagated using a specific technique. In early autumn, select some good strong vigorous shoots and

Purple Bananas

Ensete ventricosa 'Maurellii' does not easily sucker and cannot be grown from seed so is normally commercially produced by tissue culture. However there is an alternative technique that often works for the amateur gardener. A mature plant is decapitated down to a stump, almost at ground level, and the centre scooped out with a knife, aiming to actually remove the growing point. This plant is then kept warm, around 16°C (60°F) and not too moist, and the result will usually be a crop of young suckers that can be removed and grown on.

Plugs

Plugs are small partly grown plants, available in the spring months either from garden centres or by mail order. The plug trade has become quite sophisticated, and you will find many different types available. Although in some ways it does take away some of the skill and satisfaction of propagation, it does mean that you can reliably grow batches of many exotic plants without the tricky bits. It also usually means that you don't need to heat your greenhouse as early or as much as you would if you were propagating from seed or cuttings. Many of the familiar plants we have spoken about such as *Iresine*, purple fountain grass, *Plumbago*, *Alternanthera*, begonia, coleus, *Phygelius*, *Pelargonium*, *Impatiens*, *Ipomoea*, *Lantana*, *Plectranthus* and a whole host more – even bananas – are available. Plants from plugs will usually grow very fast, and you will not need to start them until mid to late Spring and they will still be ready for planting out in your garden in early Summer.

Three's Company

With some plants that are a little straggly, you can get a more chunky plant by potting three seedlings, plugs or rooted cuttings close together in the same pot. Treat as one to get a good bushy plant. Millet 'Purple Majesty' and other grasses from seed, *Abutilon megapotanicum* 'Variegatum', *Lobelia* 'Queen Victoria'

A mature plant of the purple banana that has been decapitated and encouraged to produce suckers which can be grown on as new plants.

from seed, *Bidens* cultivars, *Tradescantia* and *Verbena bonariense* are all plants that benefit from growing with company. You can try others.

Growing on

Whether you have rooted your own cuttings, grown seedlings, or bought plugs, you will need to nurture them to a suitable size for planting out. This is one of the most exciting times, as you view trays of chunky new plants bursting with growth and all the promise of the coming summer. Most spring raised plants will be finished in a 9–10cm (3½–4in) pot. Growing on should take place in an even temperature, depending

Potting on is an essential process to give young plants more space and the nutrition to allow them to fully develop before planting out.

on the plant, but often around 10°C (50°F) for many species. After about three weeks, the nutrients in many types of compost will have been exhausted, and you should supplement this with a regular liquid feed.

Plants produced early in the season or from autumn propagation will need potting on to larger pots to ensure growth continues and to produce maximum sized plants. Plants such as *Abutilon*, *Sparmannia*, *Plumbago* or *Brugmansia* should also be trained against a cane, tying in the main stem to encourage vertical growth. As sideshoots develop you can pinch these to create a nice tight pillar of growth.

The care of a greenhouse full of exotics is fairly straightforward but it does require determination and

regular attention. Greenhouses require daily maintenance, throughout most of the year. Certain automatic features are possible, but they require monitoring and checking. Managing a greenhouse full of exotics is all about creating the ideal environment for the plants you are growing. This involves controlling the heat, light, ventilation and humidity. The plants you will be growing will probably also vary considerably in their requirements, and it is down to your skill to try and get the best conditions for each.

Temperature and Humidity

Firstly the temperature should be controlled as evenly as possible. Make sure that heaters operate efficiently at night time and that ventilators are opened early on warm days. A closed greenhouse can quickly get very hot, early on a summer's day. Ventilating a greenhouse also provides a fresh source of air for plants, which need carbon dioxide to grow. In winter it is beneficial to provide a crack of ventilation, whenever possible, to avoid a build up of humidity, which often results in diseases such as botrytis.

Humidity is also of importance and will depend on the plants you are growing; bananas, cannas and gingers like to grow in a much damper atmosphere than cacti or succulents. Humidity is easily increased by damping down the floors of the greenhouse with a hose. Damping down also helps to cool a greenhouse in hot weather. By contrast in the winter, we would normally aim for a drier atmosphere to avoid disease.

Light

Light is a vital consideration for plants and particularly many exotic species, which will have originated in sunny climates. Without adequate levels, plants grow poorly or even die. So even if you heat a greenhouse in winter, plants will not grow unless there is enough light. This means that it is important to keep the greenhouse glass clean in winter to allow the maximum amount of winter sunshine to reach your plants. If you have electricity in your greenhouse and wish to grow plants over winter, it may be worth investing in special grow lights. These are particularly valuable set above propagating areas, where you are producing new seedlings and young fragile plants. Plants such as *Coleus* that have high light requirements will really benefit from the extra light.

In late spring and summer it is vital to shade a greenhouse to avoid excessively high temperatures and sunscorch. This can be done with purpose made blinds, plastic mesh or with a coating of a special greenhouse shading paint, which can be washed off in the winter. Never use emulsion paint for this job as it remains permanently.

Watering and Feeding

Giving plants adequate water for growth without drowning them is also especially important in the greenhouse. In general far more plants are killed by overwatering than underwatering. You should always wait until the compost is looking or feeling dry and then give each pot a thorough soaking. This may need to be daily in midsummer but less than once a week in winter. Hard and fast rules for watering cannot be given and you must check each plant to assess its water requirements.

Most exotics are fast growing and feeding is important, as roots in pots are restricted and the nutrients in the compost are soon exhausted. Under glass you will generally use liquid feed, or possibly slow-release fertilizers incorporated at the potting stage. Generally foliage plants need a feed high in nitrogen, and flowering plants need one with a high potassium (potash) content. All feeds should be used at the manufacturer's recommended rates.

Hardening off

The plants that you are producing in your greenhouse will mostly be frost tender and so cannot go outside into the borders until early summer when all danger of frost has passed. In the weeks leading up to that time, you need to acclimatize your plants to the tougher conditions outside. Hardening off involves increasingly opening the ventilators and door of your greenhouse, initially daytimes and eventually day and night. Ideally, move as many of your plants outdoors in their pots and containers for the last week or so before planting. In this way, you will minimize the check to growth which comes from moving plants directly from a greenhouse to the garden. Any very tender leafy

A selection of exotic plants growing on in the greenhouses at the Cotswold Wildlife Park, ready for planting out into the borders in early summer.

plants, such as bananas, ferns or houseplants will need shading from bright sunshine using horticultural fleece. If during this final hardening off period there is a sudden warning of overnight frost, you can also use fleece to provide minimal protection from low temperatures.

Never rush to plant out tender exotics in early summer. Always wait until they are properly hardened off, when you are fairly sure there will be no more frosts and the soil is warm. A chilly wet spring will leave the soil cold and exotic plants will fail to thrive. Waiting for a few days until a sunny spell has dried and warmed the soil, will enable young roots to rapidly reestablish.

Pests and Diseases

Exotic plants are not particularly prone to pests or diseases, but problems are more likely to occur with plants that are growing in greenhouses. It is especially annoying to have grown a superb batch of plants and find them decimated by pests. You should be particularly alert to problems during the spring months, as the temperatures rise and the light levels increase. There is now a very limited range of pesticides that are available for use by the amateur gardener, and so you may wish to consider the use of biological controls. This involves the use of living predators and parasites which can be introduced to a greenhouse to naturally reduce the pest. They are not particularly cheap but are available by mail order, easy to use and there is of course no risk of toxicity.

Leaf Pests

Whitefly is an annoying pest which can occur on almost any plants, but *Brugmansia*, *Abutilon*, *Fuchsia*, *Melianthus* and *Lantana* are particularly prone to attack. Unchecked, they will spread rapidly, weakening plants and causing sticky honeydew and sooty mould. They can be controlled by the use of soft soap preparations or the biological control *Encarsia*.

Lantanas are particularly prone to whitefly when grown under glass over the winter and spring months.

Cannas, *Brugmansia*, bananas and other exotics may be attacked by red spider mites; this condition is tricky to see as the creatures are microscopic and live under the leaves. They cause foliage to become progressively yellow and then brown as the creatures remove the sap from the leaves. They are deterred, although not controlled, by increasing humidity with regular damping down. Chemical control is difficult, and so you may wish to try biological control, which in this case is by a creature called *Phytoseilus*.

Aphids, or greenfly as they are often called, will attack a wide range of plants, causing a weakening of growth, sticky honeydew and again black sooty mould. Aphids also spread viruses, so their control is essential. Regular sprays of soft soap or other pesticides will reduce the populations, as will biological controls.

Mealy bugs may occur on overwintered stock plants, and leaf miner may occasionally appear. Slugs may be a problem in an old glasshouse but are more likely to be a nuisance outside in the garden.

Root Pests

The root systems of plants in pots may be affected by either vine weevils or sciarid fly larvae. Vine weevils are becoming increasingly prevalent and may unwittingly be imported to your greenhouse in the root systems of new plants from commercial nurseries. The affected plants will show poor growth and then eventually collapse and die. On inspecting the roots, you will find fat white grubs that have eaten all the roots. At this stage it is too late. It is important to check the root system of new plants and also any that are unexpectedly failing to thrive.

The larvae of the sciarid fly produce similar symptoms but on inspection you will find minute threadlike worms amongst the dying roots. Look out for silvery trails on the surface of the compost and clouds of small black flies that move fast. Chemical and biological controls are available for both, although prevention is better than cure. Some gardeners have had success by letting infected plants dry a little and then placing half a cut potato on the compost surface. This attracts the larvae which can then be destroyed.

Diseases

The most common disease that is likely to occur with exotics in a glasshouse is botrytis, which is likely to make an appearance in damp conditions over winter or during propagation, particularly if conditions aren't ideal. It can attack almost any part of the plant, causing it to rot and go mouldy. Fungicides are available, but prevention is better, making sure that you provide the right conditions for your plants and removing all dead leaves and other debris as it occurs. Good greenhouse hygiene and careful ventilation will help to avoid this problem.

Damping off disease is a problem that particularly affects young seedlings, which suddenly wilt, topple over and die. It is caused by various fungi that are often present in dirty conditions. Seed trays and pots should always be washed before use, and new clean compost should always be used. Water from water butts and tanks should never be used in a greenhouse as this is often infected with various plant diseases. A fungicide can be used as a preventative drench when watering.

Look out for symptoms such as these on cannas, indicating that the plant is badly infected with virus and must be destroyed.

PLANTING AND GROWING

So now it's showtime! You've decided to try exotic gardening, maybe bought a few plants. You will now need the ideal location to display them and grow them to perfection for exhibiting to your friends and visitors. This chapter will look at site preparation, cultivation, planting and the various jobs needed throughout the year to keep your garden looking at its best and protect your plants from one year to the next.

Preparing for Exotics

In a small garden, you may not have much choice as to where to grow your exotics, and it may well be that your whole plot will become an exotic garden. However if you have a large enough garden you will be able to choose the ideal spot for an exotic display. Shelter is probably the most important thing for exotics, so choose a location that is at least partially enclosed by existing planting but that has a fairly open sunny aspect. Most of the summer exotics, such as cannas and colourful foliage, prefer full sun to perform at their best. However small your plot, include at least some hardy exotics, such as bamboos and the other plants featured in Chapter 2, to add to the effect and provide a leafy skeleton.

Borders against brick walls are ideal, as the walls absorb warmth during the day and radiate this back overnight, which gives extra protection to tender

OPPOSITE PAGE: **A good summer display such as this in the walled garden at the University of Nottingham is down to a creative choice of plants and good cultivation.**

plants positioned nearby. However the soil is often dry, so extra irrigation may be needed. Avoid sites at the bottom of a slope. Although these may be sun traps in summer, they can also be frost pockets in winter, as cold air flows down a slope and is trapped at the bottom. The best site for an exotic garden is an open south-facing slope. This will be warm and get the majority of sunshine throughout the year, allowing cold air to drain away during the winter.

Soil Preparation

Most exotic plants grow vigorously and respond best to a well-prepared and rich soil. If the site is infested with weeds or covered by turf, you will need to attempt clearance of all green growth before cultivating and planting. During the summer months, this is best done by means of the herbicide known as glyphosate, which is very effective on perennial weeds but relatively safe to use. It only works on green tissues, so is not effective when weeds are dormant. During the winter months, the only real way of getting rid of perennial weeds is to methodically fork through the soil, removing every trace of root. Hard work!

Traditional preparation by deep digging and incorporation of organic matter is essential. You can use farmyard manure, garden compost or recycled green waste – whatever is available – and mix this well in with the soil during cultivation. Many exotics need good drainage, and so it may be necessary to improve this. Break up any compacted sub-soil to make sure that excess water can drain away. The addition of sand or grit will also improve surface drainage and ensure that air can get to the roots.

A vibrant mix of hardy and tender exotics such as this depends on a healthy soil, good cultivation and adequate moisture and nutrition.

Ideally leave the soil to weather and then break down any remaining clods to create a level fairly fine tilth just before planting. If you are planting hardy exotics during the winter months, then use a high-phosphate slow-release fertilizer such as Enmag or the traditional bonemeal, both at about 90g/m^2 (3oz/yd^2). Plantings made during the spring or summer months will benefit more from a balanced fertilizer such as the all-purpose Growmore 7:7:7, which is normally used at a rate of 60g/m^2 (2oz/yd^2). Fertilizers should be raked into the soil well before any planting takes place.

Unless you are buying a new house and garden, you're unlikely to have much choice regarding the soil for an exotic garden. However, it must be said that the greatest level of success is likely when growing on a light sandy soil or a well-drained loam. Such soils will tend to drain well and stay warmer. They should be enriched with organic matter to improve their water-holding ability. By comparison, clay soils will be rich in nutrients and hold moisture well in the summer but will tend to be badly drained and stay cold in the winter. They are less preferable for exotics and unsuitable for plants such as succulents, which require perfect drainage. Improve with organic matter and sharp sand or grit. Sharp sand from the builder's merchant is adequate, or ideally use Cornish grit, which is more expensive. Never use builder's soft sand, which will compact.

Buying Exotics

Shopping for plants for a new exotic garden can be great fun but also very expensive, and there are many different places where you can source exciting plants. Exotic gardening is an ongoing process (maybe an addiction?) and most people involved will want to continue expanding their collection of plants and trying new species. This means there is inevitably a real element of impulse buying!

Many of the hardy exotics described in this book can be obtained at garden centres, local nurseries or DIY stores. You don't need to pay fancy prices for shrubs such as *Fatsia, Pittosporum, Phormium, Yucca* and such like. In particular if you want large specimens of these, do shop around and you may even be able to do a deal with a grower if you are buying enough.

In recent years a major trade has developed in the importation of exotic specimen plants such as bamboos, palms, olive trees, succulents and other exotics. Many wholesale nurseries will have a cash-and-carry facility for individual purchases. Sales of such specimens also appear all over the place, in markets, through the internet or even as temporary outlets in disused filling stations. If you want large specimens such as palms, shop around for them from outlets such as these, where you are likely to get the best prices.

The specialist nurseries are probably some of the most exciting places to buy exotic plants. Throughout the UK there are hundreds of small nurseries specializing in all sorts of unusual plants. You will find nurseries that specialize in palms, New Zealand plants, cannas, bananas, gingers, phormiums and many more. There are also those nurseries that are a one-stop shop for the exotic garden, where you will be able to find many of the plants described here. At the end of this book you will find a list of them. A visit to any of these is an intoxicating experience, as you hop from one treasure to another, rapidly filling your trolley with exciting purchases.

Many specialist nurseries also attend rare plant fairs, which are held throughout the spring and summer. These are well worth visiting, as you may well discover unusual plants in small quantities, not available elsewhere. There is also the added bonus of advice from the nurseryman who has grown them.

The internet is also a valuable source of exotic plants, as some small growers do not open to the public and only sell via mail-order. Many large

A wide range of exotic plants is now available, many of them imported, such as this fine specimen of *Brahea armata*, the Mexican blue palm.

nurseries also have an online ordering procedure. It is also well worth checking eBay for unusual plants and seeds, particularly in the spring and early summer months. All sorts of plants, including bananas, are often available. The publication *The Plant Finder* will also help you source rare plants and is available online as well as in book form.

Importing Exotics

When on holiday abroad it can be so tempting to bring home plants that have caught your attention, but sadly it is not quite so simple. Within the European

Many brightly coloured versions of *Phormium tenax*, the New Zealand flax are available, most of which are fairly hardy.

Community, it is technically acceptable to import limited quantities of plants that are 'visibly free from signs of pest and disease and intended for personal use'. Having said that, plants are not normal holiday souvenirs, and you may well have them confiscated by customs staff who are not familiar with the rules.

To import plants from the USA or other parts of the world, you will need to be well prepared. Some overseas nurseries may be willing to carry out the necessary formalities and provide the paperwork, but it is likely to be expensive. Basically you will require a Phytosanitary Certificate, which says that the plants are healthy leaving their country of origin, and also an Import Permit. This is issued by the receiving country and would normally be arranged by the recipients and sent to the exporter in advance. Don't be tempted to smuggle in plants without the correct documentation. Without this, the customs officials will seize and destroy any plants, however rare or costly.

After you receive the plants, you will be visited by your local Plant Health Inspector, who checks that the plants are healthy. Despite this, you should always grow newly imported plants in isolation, in case any unexpected pests or diseases occur.

If you are considering the importation of plants from far-flung countries, you'll also need to make sure that they travel by the fastest possible method. It can be most frustrating to finally receive a parcel containing rare but dead plants.

Planting Exotics

If you are creating an exotic garden from scratch, you are likely to be planting some hardy exotics such as trees, shrubs, bamboos and possibly herbaceous perennials. These are best planted during the winter or early spring. At this time of year root establishment will be quick and plants can settle in, well before they have to make new growth in the following spring and summer.

With all planting, whether or not you have drawn a plan in advance, you should lay out the plants where you intend to grow them, stand back and try and imagine the effect after they have put on a few years' growth.

The layout of our exotic garden will obviously depend on the space we have available, its size shape and any existing features. Generally it is best to plant hardy exotics primarily as a background or skeleton and leave space at the front of the borders for the addition of our tender species which we will add each

ABOVE: **These tree ferns were imported as sections of dormant trunk, which have now started to produce new growths and will rapidly produce a full head.**

LEFT: **Some exotic plants can be found in strange places, such as these dormant cycads for sale in the floating flower market in Amsterdam.**

summer. Remember that many of the hardies will eventually be large shrubs or small trees. Even the smallest should be no closer to their neighbours than a metre, and specimens such as bamboos and those that make small trees should be at least 2m (7ft) apart. In the early stages this will look very sparse, but we can add to this by planting hardy groundcover plants or by interplanting with tender species.

If you have in mind planting a tree fern, they are normally purchased as dormant trunks. These will have a clear growing point at one end and obviously need the opposite end to be firmly anchored in the ground. You can quite simply dig a hole and bury the base of the stem in the ground, but you will need at least 30cm (12in) of buried stem to support a 2m (6ft) trunk. It always seems a pity to bury a large part of what you have purchased, so the alternative is to bury just 15cm (6in) and tie the trunk to a traditional tree stake. If you position this behind a tree fern's trunk, it will not be too conspicuous, and within a season or two, when the tree fern has established new roots, you can remove the stake.

The basic principle of planting exotics is just the same as with any other planting project. Dig a good size hole, loosen the subsoil, plant to the correct depth and firm in gently with your boots. Finish off a permanent planting with a mulch, which is not only attractive but retains moisture and reduces weed growth. Materials such as bark, leaf mould, good garden compost or recycled green waste all make excellent mulching materials. Coloured glass mulches are also available and may provide just the right contrast to what you are growing.

Planting Tender Exotics

You should not attempt to plant out frost-tender exotics until all danger of frost has passed in late spring. There is actually very little advantage to earlier planting. Not only do you risk damage by a late frost, but planting into a cold wet soil gives tender plants a poor start. They will tend to sit and 'sulk' and really not start growing until the soil warms up. Really soft exotics, such as cannas, can be left until early summer, and when planted into a warm soil they will romp away with vigorous growth. Don't be impatient!

Planting out summer exotics is perhaps the most exciting job in the exotic garden. For most adventurous gardeners, the real creativity comes into play as you experiment with how the different plants interact with each other, as you space them out on the border itself. Some of them such as coleus and other foliage plants will immediately be showing their display qualities, but with others, such as cannas and

The main specimens for a new display are laid out, to assess the arrangement.

TOP LEFT: **A good sized hole is dug, and the root ball of this *Cordyline* is carefully positioned.**

TOP RIGHT: **The soil is carefully filled in around the rootball and firmed in place.**

MIDDLE LEFT: **Smaller plants such as this *Alocasia* are more easily planted using a hand trowel.**

MIDDLE RIGHT: **New plantings should be watered in thoroughly to settle the soil around the roots.**

BOTTOM RIGHT: **Slug pellets being applied as a protection to soft young plants.**

dahlias, you will have to use your imagination and conjure up a picture of them in full display by midsummer. It's a fun but also skilful job, juggling with the interplay of different colours, types of foliage, speed of growth and eventual heights of all the exciting plants we are using. Remember many exotic plants can be quite boisterous, and you will need to allow enough space for them to grow and develop without smothering their better behaved neighbours. Plants such as *Colocasia* may grow to at least a metre tall, and the broad leaves may spread just as much.

From a practical point of view you will need to initially space out and plant all your really big specimens, things like bananas, *Brugmansias*, palms, *Abutilons* and anything else that is coming from a large pot. Position these, visualizing what they will look like when fully grown at the end of the summer. Stand back and look at that knee-high purple banana, imagining it towering above you, with huge glistening paddle leaves when fully grown. The planting procedure is the same as for hardy species, and when you have finished, rake out the surplus soil to get a smooth tilth for planting the smaller plants.

The next to go in are the mid-size plants, such things as cannas, gingers, *Colocasia* and grasses.

Finally position the smallest plants, in their pots, on the surface of the soil at the correct spacing. Most plants from small pots, such as *Pelargoniums*, coleus, *Alternanthera* and other bedding plants, will need to be planted 20–30cm (9–12in) apart, which will result in a good even cover of foliage and flower when fully grown.

When you are happy with the final appearance, plant them using a trowel, firming in gently as you go. When each area is complete, water in thoroughly using a sprinkler or a hosepipe with a fine rose. Do be sure to thoroughly soak, so that the water percolates right down to the roots and doesn't just dampen the surface. Depending on weather conditions, you will probably have to repeat this every few days until your new plants are well established. Any lush foliage is a temptation to slugs and snails that can rapidly decimate tender new plants, so always use a slug treatment around all new plantings. You can either use traditional slug pellets or alternatively there is a biological control available.

Occasionally there are late unexpected frosts which can be devastating, browning the foliage of freshly planted exotics and sometimes killing them. If you have warning of this, try to provide some light protection in advance. Use garden fleece, old net curtains, light sheeting or even newspapers to loosely cover tender plants. Such a covering will usually be enough to protect from a light frost. If the worst happens and plants become frosted, try to hose them over with cold water before the sun has a chance to thaw them. Usually cold water will allow a slow enough thaw to prevent undue damage. It's an old trick but it works.

Summer Care

Exotic gardening is not particularly demanding in the summer, although there will be some tasks you will need to do. If conditions are warm and moist, exotic plantings will astonish you with their speed of growth. Not surprisingly, weeds will also grow at the same rate, and you will need to control these by hand weeding or by hoeing to ensure they do not compete with your precious exotics for valuable food and moisture.

Nearly all exotic plantings respond well to water, and so if conditions are dry you should be sure to irrigate thoroughly to prevent growth being stressed. Don't forget that tree ferns should never be allowed to dry out; in particular the fibrous trunks must be kept moist. The taller *Lobelias* should also not be allowed to get too dry or they will tend to wilt and kink.

From about six weeks after planting it can also be useful to add extra feed. You can use a granular feed such as Growmore, gently sprinkled around your plants at a rate of about 60g/m^2 (2oz/yd^2), tickled into the surface and then well irrigated in. Alternatively you can use a liquid feed, and some proprietary brands now offer their own diluters which make the job so much easier. Remember lush foliage plants such

Over the summer months, if conditions are dry be sure to keep exotic plants well watered in order to maximize growth.

as bananas, *Colocasia* and palms really need a feed which is high in nitrogen. To encourage flowers, for example dahlias or cannas, it is preferable to use a high potash feed. However with a mixed planting, a good balanced general purpose liquid feed will usually be acceptable.

A few plants, such as dahlias may need staking to ensure they do not flop over. Dahlias, cannas and other large flowered plants will also need dead-heading to encourage more blooms. Also trim off dying and untidy leaves on species such as bananas which readily get scruffy. Sometimes coleus will try to flower, but the flowers are insignificant so always pinch out the buds to encourage a fresh flush of coloured foliage.

You can continue to indulge your artistic skills throughout the summer as the display changes. Inevitably as certain plants mature and finish their display or possibly fail to thrive, gaps will appear. Don't think of them as problems but more as opportunities to add something new. Use pots of late produced bedding, or maybe summer bulbs such as lilies. You can either plant them properly or just tuck them in so that the pots are hidden by other foliage. Throughout summer, garden centres are always

Keep an eye on your local garden centre for interesting plants such as these colourful calla lilies, which make useful fillers for any mid-summer gaps.

stocked with masses of instant colour, so if you need plants or inspiration, this is the place to go. Above all, do find time to enjoy your exotic garden in the summer. Wander round it, sit and gaze at it, share it with friends – all too soon it will be winter again.

Autumn in the Exotic Garden

Exotic gardens tend to get increasingly dramatic towards the end of summer, and some can be looking at their best right into early autumn. Bananas will be big and lush, cannas and dahlias full of flower, *Ricinus* towering over flowing carpets of coloured foliage and scramblers struggling through everything in jungle-like abandon. In fact, the display of many exotics will stay looking good right the way through until the first frost.

However as a good gardener you will need to start making preparations for the coming winter, to ensure your garden and exotic plants are going to survive for next year. Depending on what you are growing, you may need to do some autumn propagation. In Chapter 6 we spoke about the cuttings that you will need to take; early autumn is a good time for things like coleus, *Iresine*, *Pelargonium*, *Abutilon* and *Brugmansia*.

Lifting Stock

If there are stock plants or specimens, such as the purple banana, that you want to keep till next year but are too tender to stay outside, then they should be carefully dug from the borders, potted and taken to a frost-free greenhouse, well in advance of the first frost. Tidy up such plants, removing any dead leaves and shaking off excess soil. Pot them up in the smallest suitable pot, using potting compost and watering well. Plants such as pelargoniums or fuchsias that will be used as stock plants for the spring, or tall specimen plants, may be trimmed back to a framework to save space.

Cannas, gingers, dahlias and other bulbous plants can be left in the ground until the first frost. As soon as the frost browns the foliage, trim back the stems to about 15cm (6in). Carefully dig the clumps, being sure not to damage any of the fleshy roots. Gently shake or wash off excess soil. Leave some soil to avoid the roots drying out excessively over the winter. Dahlias are often stored for a short while upside down to allow the remaining moisture to drain from the succulent stems. Cannas and dahlias must be very carefully labelled, as it will be impossible to separately identify until they flower again next summer.

All of these 'roots' should then be packed together into containers such as deep boxes containing peat, bark or old used potting soil. The containers need to

This tender banana has been carefully lifted with a good rootball and will be potted up before returning to a heated greenhouse for the winter.

This specimen *Agave* has got too big to dig up in the autumn and so is being protected by its own small in situ greenhouse.

PLANTS TO PROTECT FOR WINTER

Aloe – various species
Agave americana
Amicia zygomeris
Beschorneria septentrionalis and *B. yuccoides*
Brahea armata
Butia capitata
Cycas revoluta
Grevillea – various species
Nerium oleander
Phoenix canariensis
Pseudopanax – various species
Restios
Pittosporum tobira
Schefflera – various species

go into a frost-free store, which can be under the bench of a heated greenhouse, an insulated garage or a warm cellar. Over the winter months check them regularly. Any signs of mould should be treated with a fungicide, such as green sulphur. If the storage material starts to get very dry, you should very gently damp it over with a light spray of water. You do not want your stored plants to desiccate.

Mulching and Wrapping

Some gardeners decide to leave cannas, gingers, dahlias or other tender roots in the ground over winter; this is an acceptable alternative treatment that is successful in all but the coldest winters. If you decide to do this, cover over the rooting zone with a good thick mulch of compost or shredded bark. This should make a good cushion at least 15cm (6in) thick,

A large multi-stemmed plant of _Musa basjoo_, wrapped with straw and with a plastic roof to protect it from winter cold and rain.

double layer of horticultural fleece. The root zone is mulched to protect the roots from frost. Cycads can be treated similarly and _Fascicularia_ can benefit from a tuft of straw in its crown.

Some exotic gardeners have also had success protecting succulents such as _Agaves_ by supporting panes of glass above the plants or by constructing small temporary 'greenhouses' with timber and plastic sheeting. These shed off excess water, keeping the crowns, soil and foliage just a little bit drier and marginally warmer.

Many exotic gardeners also have conservatories or porches which may be suitable for overwintering tender plants. If you do not have greenhouse space for all the plants you would like to protect, you could also gamble by moving plants to a shed or garage. Although conditions may not be ideal, and light will be severely limited, you may be able to protect plants over the coldest months of the year, moving them back outside as soon as you can. Any potted plants left outside are more exposed than those in the ground. You may like to move tender plants such as palms closer to your house, where they will have a little more shelter. You can also wrap the pots in bubble wrap to keep the root zone warmer.

Quite sizeable plants of the hardy banana, _Musa basjoo_ and also _M. sikkimensis_ can be protected in situ by a simple technique. At the end of the summer, trim off all the green foliage to the top of the 'stems' – this may seem drastic but new leaves will grow quickly next year. A tube of wire netting, about 45cm (18in) in diameter, stapled to a tree stake works well with a single stem. This is then stuffed with straw making sure the banana stem is well within the straw. The structure needs to be finished off with a 'hat' made from a plastic bag to keep the rain off the top. Don't be tempted to wrap the whole plant in plastic as this will 'sweat' and the plant likely to rot. Larger, multi-stemmed plants will need a bigger structure. This can be more wire netting stretched around four tree stakes or a more substantial construction made from wooden pallets. Either can be topped off with a sheet of exterior grade plywood to shed the rain.

Such protection needs to stay in place until mid to late spring, according to the area and weather. It is

extending over the area where you expect the roots to be. Mulching is a good technique to combine with other protection for almost any tender plants as it will keep the root system warm, and even if the top is cut down by frost, the roots may survive and the plant regenerate.

Any young palms or other slightly tender shrubs can be given some protection by wrapping with horticultural fleece or sacking, tied around a simple framework of bamboo canes. Leave the top open to allow a good circulation of air. Figs are hardy, but wrap if you want to protect the embryonic fruits for next year.

Tree ferns can be protected by stuffing handfuls of straw into the growing points. In colder areas the complete wrapping of tree ferns is recommended. The fronds should be tied upright with straw packed in the centre, and the whole bundle wrapped in a then removed and the plant tidied up. Watch out for mice and over wintering wasps. A generous dressing of a balanced fertilizer is beneficial and give it a thorough watering if conditions are dry. The new leaves that quickly appear will be those which were partly formed and encased in the leaf sheaths that made up the false stem last year.

Winter and Spring Work

The winter months are not the most exciting for exotic gardeners, and many tend to hibernate just like the plants they grow. However there will be jobs to do, such as pruning hardy exotics, preparing soil and planting new stock. In the event of heavy snow, knock as much as possible from foliage of palms and other evergreens to reduce damage.

Pruning is a skilled job that should always be done to improve the appearance of the plant, reduce its size or to encourage its display. Use sharp secateurs or a pruning saw. Never, ever use hedge-trimmers to prune shrubs. They wreck the natural shapes and often remove the growths which are needed for flowering. Plants do not usually need pruning unless there is a problem. If they block paths, doors or windows, prune them, but otherwise leave them alone. Never be tempted to prune spiky plants as the shape can easily be ruined.

Most exotic gardeners are ambitious and will want next year's display to look even better, so this is the time to review the success of last year's plantings and prepare for next year. Be ruthless and dig out those plants that have not performed well or have exceeded their allotted space. Winter is also a good time to peruse the catalogues and search out new species, order seeds and plants for next year's display and generally dream of summer.

Most spring work in the exotic garden will take place in your greenhouse, propagating and growing new plants for the coming summer. However there

Many exotic-looking plants can be amazingly tough and will tolerate quite low temperatures with frost and snow.

will be some jobs to do outside in advance of the summer. All permanent plantings will benefit from a top dressing of a balanced fertilizer such as Growmore, applied at $60g/m^2$ ($2ozs/yd^2$). If possible, follow this with a mulch of good garden compost, spent mushroom compost or shredded bark. Any empty areas to be planted later should be dug over and prepared in the normal way. This is also a good time of the year to carry out the hard pruning of woody plants such as *Paulownia*, which we call stooling (*see* page 24). Check over tender plants that have been outside during the winter and cut out any dead or damaged shoots. In late spring, according to the weather, you can start to unwrap bananas and other exotics that have been protected over the winter.

EXOTIC DESIGN

Exotic gardening is fun and it's flashy. It's often big, bold and bright, making it a style of gardening that can be easily criticized for being tasteless. Even though exotic gardens may be flamboyant and even amusing, there is no reason why they should not be exquisitely designed, meticulously maintained and contain a wealth of fascinating features and stunning plants. These next two chapters will discuss exotic garden design – how to use plants to create special effects, what to put on the ground, and how you might add those extras such as sculpture, furniture or even garden buildings.

Exotic Concepts

Many of the plants described so far, such as bananas, tree ferns, cannas, the aroids and most of the summer exotics, together with hardy plants such as bamboos and architectural evergreens, create an effect that is very much an urban jungle. For most people this is the desired exotic effect. Dabbling with this style also enables so many adventurous gardeners to experiment with plants which you would not expect to grow in temperate climates. There is a huge palette of fascinating, colourful and architectural plants available, many of which are fast-growing. Good gardeners soon learn that the way in which plants are grouped together makes a great difference to the end result. Exotic gardens are often some of the most

dramatic landscapes that it is possible to create. Success or failure depends not only on good culture but also on a dramatic design.

Design does not have to involve scale plans and drawings. By all means use paper and pencil if this helps, but really design is all about imagination. The first stage is dream gardening. Close your eyes and picture your ideal garden. Maybe you will conjure up the image of somewhere special that you admire – another garden or a holiday destination, or possibly a style you favour – an exotic pool with floating lotus or a desert landscape bristling with cacti. There may be favourite plants that you'd like to grow – cannas, bananas, bamboos or whatever. Be ambitious. Imagine that riot of exotic colour that you've always fancied. All these ideas are the beginnings of a design that can take shape on paper or in your mind, and eventually as a real living exotic landscape.

Good gardens have interesting shapes. But remember that the shapes that you create, whether they be lawns, paved areas, beds or borders, need not mirror the shape of your garden. Far too many gardeners automatically put a rectangular lawn in a rectangular garden. Exotic gardens are for adventurous people, so think differently. Gardens can be formal or informal, and this applies to exotic gardens as much as any landscape. A formal layout will be based on straight lines and geometric shapes, whereas an informal design will have graceful sweeping curves and look more natural. The informal style is probably most suited to exotic gardening, but not exclusively. The much revered exotic garden at Great Dixter is based on a matrix of formal beds bisected by straight paved footpaths, but this is overlaid with a wonderfully informal confection of exotic plants.

OPPOSITE PAGE: **This exotic garden, created by Tony Hoffman in Nottingham, is simple but beautifully designed and based mainly on hardy exotics.**

These colourful exotic borders at East Ruston Old Vicarage are formal and geometric in style but contain a plethora of lush planting.

Planting Design

Although gardens are created using many materials and features, it is primarily the selection and arrangement of plants which gives an exotic garden its unique appeal. Although many of the colourful plants in the exotic garden have flowers, the majority are grown for their foliage. And despite the colourful possibilities with some, the predominant colour is green. However, there is a lot of difference and individuality about the many plants available. All plants have at least two characteristics other than colour, and these are structure and texture.

Structure is all about a plant's shape, sometimes called form – whether it is upright, rounded or spreading. Some plants have a spiky outline, whereas others may be rounded, upright or have branches that create a layered effect. When we arrange plants together in any planting display, it is useful to try and contrast one shape against another. For example a

tall, narrow, upright plant, such as bamboo, will look good contrasted against a more spreading plant such as a carpet of *Bergenia*. A rounded plant such as *Griselinia* will look good contrasted with a spiky plant such as *Phormium*. Inevitably many exotic plants have bold shapes.

Texture refers to the pattern made by a plant's leaves (and to a certain extent flowers). This may be either a small delicate grain, created by hundreds of small leaves, or a much bolder pattern created by large leaves. The surface of leaves also varies, with some being smooth and glossy and others being hairy or velvety. The edges may be smooth, rippled or serrated in some way. All these factors add to the texture and value of leaves. Many of you will be familiar with thinking about the patterns on carpets and curtains in interior design. Most of you would probably choose a plain carpet to be contrasted with patterned curtains, and in the garden it is very similar. For example, use plants such as *Pittosporum,* with its masses of tiny crinkly leaves, contrasted against something like *Tetrapanax papyrifer* with large hairy leaves. Each will enhance the other and make the overall display more interesting.

Putting plants together also involves an overview of the entire scheme, or sections of it in a big garden. A border will require a focal point – a tree or large specimen shrub. A large area will require more than one, but unless the layout is very formal, these need not be matching or symmetrically placed. So for example, a border might contain a tall *Eucalyptus* tree, a specimen bamboo and a big *Phormium tenax*. These three focal points should be spread within the border in a large triangle, not a straight row. Smaller arrangements of complimentary plants will be built up around each of these key plants. As you add other plants remember that many species look good in groups – threes, fives or other odd numbers. As an exotic gardener you will be tempted to grow a wide range of plants, but for the sake of the design, try to repeat the use of key plants. So for example, when you plant *Colocassias*, position three or more groups along your border. This repetition, or rhythm as it is sometimes called, helps to give the planting a cohesive structure.

The broad leaves of *Tetrapanax* and *Cercis* 'Forest Pansy' contrast with the smaller leaved bamboos in both the foreground and background.

The Rainforest Effect

Anyone who has been lucky enough to have visited a genuine rainforest, or just watched television documentaries, will have noticed that the plants within a rainforest are on many different levels. These are classified, starting with the forest floor, followed by the understory, then the canopy and finally the emergent layer right at the top. Such a mix of plants and wildlife may in a real rainforest extend to a height of over 45m (150ft). It is unlikely that in any temperate exotic garden you will have anywhere near that amount of growth, but the principle is useful to follow and you should try to create several different layers of interest.

For example we might well have an area which is dominated by a mature tree such as the golden-leaved *Robinia pseudoacacia* 'Frisia'. Underneath that we could have some clumps of the black bamboo,

Phyllostachys nigra and next to that a plant of the hardy banana, *Musa basjoo*. We might well have some climbing vines scrambling up through the layers. Then growing to no more than waist height we might have some gingers or cannas, and then right on the ground something creeping such as *Helychryssum, Tradescantia* or low growing coleus. Each distinct plant complements its neighbour, with diverse textures of foliage, different shapes and interest at each level.

Floorscapes

All gardens need open spaces which contrast with the denser areas of planting and practically provide areas to walk on. These may traditionally be lawns, gravel, paving or decking. Lawns are by no means essential, although they may provide just the perfect green oasis in the centre of all your lush plantings. Grass, despite being alive, is a very stark formal contrast to loose planting. It is difficult to let planting just drift into grass. Although you can plant individual specimens into lawns, it is not so easy, and they tend to look very contrived rather than natural. It is very much the way exotics were displayed back in the nineteenth century with big tufts of pampas set in the middle of mown grass. Nowadays a more informal style is usually favoured.

By contrast gravel provides a loose flexible material which can be used to create pathways through your exotic planting and open spaces of any shape. Planting doesn't need to immediately stop at the edge of gravel, as it usually does with a lawn. Individual plants can be added to gravel quite easily, or species such as grasses can be allowed to seed at the edges. In this way your planting gently flows into the gravel. The cheapest of gravels, sometimes called pea shingle, is usually a soft golden colour which weathers to a dull grey. Various other types, from white through to almost black, are available together with different colours such as a lovely dull terracotta, sold as red porphyry. With gravels, you don't need to stop at one type but can combine sweeps of different coloured or sized gravels, together with cobbles, paddle stones and boulders, all creating interest in your floorscape.

Alternatively, paving or decking might be just right for a modern, formal exotic garden. They certainly provide the best surface for hard use in areas such as

This formal Mediterranean courtyard has a range of spiky exotic plants set amongst a variety of coloured gravels, cobbles and boulders.

Decking has been used to separate this pool from the surrounding exotic planting, creating a pleasant area for relaxation on a sunny day.

access paths or outdoor dining spaces. There are numerous possibilities, but do remember that exotic gardening is a bold and expressive style so try to use materials that are not too traditional. Sections of paving can be replaced by planted blocks of groundcover or specimen plants. Decking can be broken up with areas of coloured foliage or other groundcover plants. Different levels and raised beds can be retained using steel gabions filled with cobbles or reclaimed bricks. Think different!

Footpaths should be fun too. They will inevitably have a utilitarian value, giving you access to different areas of your garden for maintenance purposes, but do also use them as design features. Create pathways through exotic planting, adding to the experience for you and your visitor. It's fun to walk under the leaves of bananas and between tall bamboos and imagine a

Brazilian rainforest. Include unexpected twists and curves, and ensure that paths have an interesting ending – a destination. The end of a footpath should lead you to a different area of the garden, out into an open space or to a focal point, a particular item of interest. Focal points can be either inanimate objects, such as a seat or an item of sculpture, or a specimen plant or a container bursting with a crescendo of plants. Whatever its nature, it needs to be something a little bit special and to be placed at the end of a footpath where it catches the eye. Well-designed gardens should have a series of focal points in key locations.

One of the most interesting devices to use in designing a garden is the element of surprise or the unexpected. So for example you are exploring an exotic garden and making your way through a very

A novel water feature powered by a small pump to give a gentle trickling waterfall and the magic of moving water.

restful grove of green bamboos and you turn a corner. At the end of the footpath there is a bright red British post box, spouting water – not quite what you'd expect in the middle of an exotic garden. Such items do much to add the ultimate 'wow' factor.

Colour Theories

Colour is important to all of us, whatever our particular preferences might be. Colour in our exotic garden is provided partly by flowering species but also by foliage plants with particularly brilliant leaves. Colour is a personal thing, and whilst some of you

may love hot vibrant colours, these may not be the personal preference for all readers of this book. Whilst the majority of plants that are recommended within this colour section will be brilliantly coloured, there is no reason why an exotic garden cannot be planted in soft pastel shades.

Some gardeners would suggest that there is no need for a colour scheme within the garden. Undeniably, colours do not seem to clash quite so much where there is also a preponderance of green leaves, brown soil and blue sky. Having said that, exotic gardens are not simply a piece of nature; they are man-made and contrived, and as such benefit from good design. Whilst we may not wish to have a rigid colour scheme for our exotic garden, we can nevertheless create some exciting effects by restricting the palette of colours we are using.

In the Victorian era, one of the most hotly debated topics in the gardening world was colour theory. Some of these principles are just as valid today. Colour schemes can be described as contrasting, where we have very different colours together, such as orange and blue or yellow and purple. Complementary colours are those that are similar, such as blue and purple or yellow and orange. Colour schemes which use contrasting colours tend to be the most powerful.

You can also create monochromatic colour schemes, using different shades of just one colour, so you might have the red flowered *Canna* 'President' with ruby-leaved Coleus 'Juliet Quartermain' and tall red and bronze *Lobelia* 'Queen Victoria'. Adding just a touch of another colour can be effective so you might include threads of *Helichrysum* 'Limelight'. Pastel shades are paler versions of almost any colour, such as pinks, sky blues, or primrose yellow, and using such colours tends to produce a quieter, more restful effect.

Within the overall scheme, we can also design small vignettes, where groups of plants have contrasting or complementary colours within a small area. So for example we might have the golden variegated *Canna* 'Striata' next to the red-leaved *Iresine*, the golden-leaved *Pelargonium* 'Vancouver Centennial' and the spiky purple fountain grass. This little group makes a planting scheme all on its own and could well be

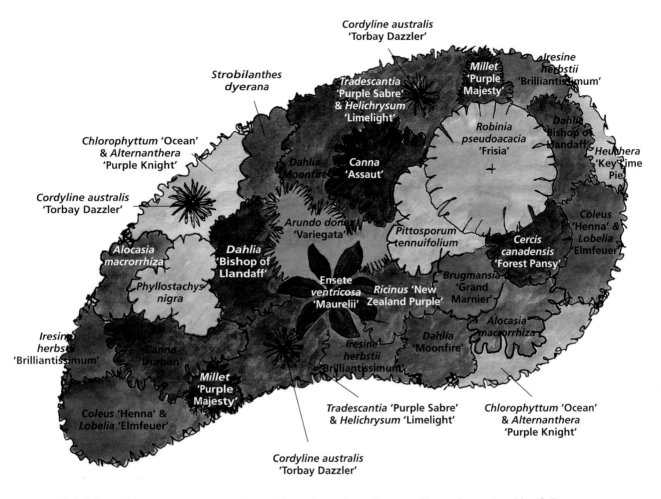

Cordyline australis 'Torbay Dazzler'

Strobilanthes dyerana

Tradescantia 'Purple Sabre' & Helichrysum 'Limelight'

Millet 'Purple Majesty'

Iresine herbstii 'Brilliantissimum'

Chlorophyttum 'Ocean' & Alternanthera 'Purple Knight'

Robinia pseudoacacia 'Frisia'

Dahlia 'Bishop of Llandaff'

Heuchera 'Key Lime Pie'

Cordyline australis 'Torbay Dazzler'

Dahlia 'Moonfire'

Canna 'Assaut'

Coleus 'Henna' & Lobelia 'Elmfeuer'

Alocasia macrorrhiza

Dahlia 'Bishop of Llandaff'

Arundo donax 'Variegata'

Pittosporum tenuifolium

Cercis canadensis 'Forest Pansy'

Phyllostachys nigra

Ensete ventricosa 'Maurelii'

Ricinus 'New Zealand Purple'

Brugmansia 'Grand Marnier'

Alocasia macrorrhiza

Iresine herbstii 'Brilliantissimum'

Canna 'Durban'

Iresine herbstii 'Brilliantissimum'

Dahlia 'Moonfire'

Millet 'Purple Majesty'

Coleus 'Henna' & Lobelia 'Elmfeuer'

Tradescantia 'Purple Sabre' & Helichrysum 'Limelight'

Chlorophyttum 'Ocean' & Alternanthera 'Purple Knight'

Cordyline australis 'Torbay Dazzler'

This bright and extrovert summer scheme blatantly explores the use of hot colours. A golden foliage Robinia, contrasted with a purple-leaved Cercis and a group of black bamboo, provide a permanent skeleton. To that is added a confection of tender summer colour, including the brilliant and lush foliage of Iresine, coleus, cordylines, variegated Arundo donax and Alocasia. Dahlias, tall red lobelia, angel's trumpets and canna provide flower power.

either the contents of a large planter or a pocket in a large border of exotics. Such a group could be separated from the next colour cameo with an evergreen or something neutral such as silver variegated grass. White and silver are neutral colours which can be used in almost any combination, but they are particularly useful as foils for darker colours such as deep blue, rich purple and dark maroon.

Some of the most exciting displays are those where two or more plants are chosen to complement each other intimately. So for example if you have purple fountain grass and the rich ruby foliage of Iresine, you can either use them in two separate groups or mix them together for a startling two-tone and double storey effect. Don't also forget the value of climbers at this point, not just for walls and trellises but to scramble through other plants. The orange flowers of Ipomoea lobata looks great growing through something with dark foliage such as Dodonea viscosa 'Purpurea'.

Be adventurous, mix together orange and maroon, lemon yellow and cerise pink or lavender and bright scarlet. Maybe you have some vivid purple dahlias, some bright orange *Kniphofia* and some tall maroon cannas – not the obvious bedfellows maybe, but try them together. If the result is a success, build on this next year, and if a grinding clash, try something different. Probably the greatest exponent of colour in recent times has been Christopher Lloyd. His use of colour, not only in his exotic plantings but also throughout his garden at Great Dixter, was daring, to say the least. Anyone wanting to more about colour in the garden should read his fascinating and beautifully illustrated book, *Colour for Adventurous Gardeners*.

ABOVE: **Brilliant scarlet coleus are contrasted with the purple foliage of** *Heuchera* **'Liquorice', a purple banana and the silvery threads of** *Festuca glauca.*

LEFT: **The bronze foliage of this** *Canna* **'Intrigue' is best displayed in brilliant sunshine to make the most of its rich colourings.**

Light and Shade

Unfortunately none of us have control over one factor which has a major influence on our exotic garden and colours in particular – that is of course the presence, or sadly too often the absence, of sunshine. In designing our exotic garden we can nevertheless plan our plantings in such a way that when the sun does shine, its effects are maximized.

Always position plants such as dark-leaved cannas

or purple-leaved *Cercis* 'Forest Pansy' so that the sunshine can glow through the foliage. Such deep opulent colours as these, which are rich in intensity, look fabulous in catalogues but can sometimes be disappointing when used in the garden, as they are just too dark. If they are to be effective, rich dark colours must be used in situations which receive full sunlight and then they will absolutely glow. The same could be said of the various plants which are described as black. This will include plants such as *Colocassia* 'Black Magic', *Coleus* 'Black Prince', *Phormium* 'Platt's Black', *Canna* 'Black Knight' and *Ipomoea* 'Blackie'. All are fascinating plants but should be used sparingly and mixed with brilliant or light colours and in full sunshine.

Remember the value of shadows. On a bright sunny day, plants such as palms with an interesting foliage shape will cast clear shadows on surrounding surfaces. Such a pattern will be lost amongst the busyness of other foliage but will show up clearly on grass or a smooth surface such as gravel or paving. Although we cannot stop the rain and turn on the sun on a drizzly summer's day, we can make sure that our garden looks at its best when the sun does shine.

In designing a planting scheme we need to be constantly aware of all these factors: height, structure, texture, rhythm, colour and light. By using these and contrasting the different characteristics, as we put together different plants we can build fascinating blocks of exotic foliage and flowers.

Don't be afraid to include peculiar plants for the sheer fun of it. There are all sorts of bizarre members of the plant world which fit well in an exotic garden. The great plantsman E.A. Bowles had what he called his 'lunatic asylum' where he collected his maniacs, plants with unusual features. Use the quirky twisted stems of *Corylus* 'Red Majestic' amongst your background planting. Try a container with some devil's claw, *Probiscidea althaeifolia* for its ugly black seedpods. Then there are those plants that have 'party pieces' such as the sensitive plant, *Mimosa pudica,* which neatly folds up its leaves when touched, or *Dictamnus albus,* which produces volatile oils and can be set on fire on a warm evening. All part of the theatre of an exotic garden.

Exotic Water Features

Water in any garden adds another dynamic and no more so than in the exotic garden. Picture a luxuriant tropical landscape with palms and bananas flourishing around a dark and mysterious pond. Add the intense highlights of tropical water lilies and you have the very essence of an exotic garden. Water should however always be an integral part of your design, blending in with the style of your garden – its shapes, the floorscape, any materials used and the overall planting.

Not only does water add another dimension to our landscape, but it also provides the ideal growing conditions for many exotics which prefer a damp environment. Plants such as *Gunnera, Rheum, Zantedeschia,* water cannas and many of the other aroids all thrive in the damp soil at the edge of a water feature. Water also attracts wildlife, and you can expect to see an increase in bird life, insects such as dragonflies, and amphibians such as frogs and toads.

Pools can be constructed in a number of ways. Concrete is undoubtedly the most durable but will also be the most expensive and inflexible material to handle. Prefabricated fibreglass pools are available in numerous sizes and shapes and may well be suitable for what you want. However the cheapest and probably most adaptable of all materials is a butyl liner which can be adapted to any shape and depth of pool. Most exotic pools will probably be informal, and butyl will mould smoothly to curves. Construction of pools is a detailed subject and beyond the scope of this book, but be sure to construct your pool deep enough for fish if you want them and with a series of shelves to allow for aquatics at different levels.

Aquatic Exotics

From the extensive array of aquatic plants available to us, there are many that are particularly suitable for the exotic garden. Some of the best marginal plants must be the water cannas developed from *Canna glauca,* all of which have narrow foliage and small flowers – 'Endeavour' is deep reddish pink, 'Erebus' is a pale pink and 'Ra' is a soft yellow. They are treated much the same as terrestrial cannas but grown in aquatic baskets and placed at the edge of the pool, with up to 15cm (6in) of water above the roots. Some gardeners have had equal success with growing other vigorous cultivars such as 'Wyoming' as water cannas. The blue-flowered *Thalia dealbata* is another good exotic marginal, as is *Cyperus papyrus*.

The adventurous may want to try tropical waterlilies such as *Nymphaea caerulea,* or various forms of *Nelumbo,* the sacred lotus. The flowers are exquisite and many have a heavenly perfume. However in order to grow them, you will need a warm pond or to use the heated planters that are now available for aquatics such as these. There is also the giant *Victoria amazonica,* if you want a real aquatic challenge.

Thermoplanters are specialist planters with an integrated heating element that keeps the container warm at all times. Some are intended to be used as a patio planter to keep the roots of tender potted exotics warm. Others are designed to be used underwater as aquatic containers for tropical water lilies. You will obviously need a suitable external electricity supply for these to function safely.

Water hyacinth, *Eichhornia crassipes* and water lettuce, *Pistia stratiotes* are both floating species,

This show garden features an exotic pool and thatched loggia set amongst colourful cannas, lush tree ferns and palms.

usually readily available from aquatic suppliers in the summer, but remember they are not frost hardy so will need to be taken into the greenhouse in the winter or bought afresh each year.

As well as still water, there is of course the possibility of movement, with all manner of fountains and waterfalls possible, with the use of a submersible pump and with some imagination and ingenuity. The New Zealand Garden at Mount Edgcumbe in the UK features a 'geyser' that shoots a great column of water into the air without warning, to the surprise and delight of passing visitors. A recent flower show garden featured an ingenious waterfall and fountain made from an old washing machine – possibly not the most decorative object but certainly a great talking point and a high score for recycling. Exotic gardening is always distinctly tongue in cheek, so there is no reason why you cannot also have fun with a water feature.

Ongoing Design

Remember that good gardens are never finished. An exotic landscape, like any other, is a growing, changing, dynamic creation which will be different every year as plants grow and their interaction alters. Some plants may die, others become too large or, quite simply, you may tire of some. Don't be afraid of change. Dig out those plants that have become less valuable and try something new. Make notes each summer of what you need to change the next winter or of ideas you have for the next season.

Cyperus papyrus, **the ancient Egyptian source of paper, is an excellent exotic-looking aquatic plant, easily grown from seed.**

POTS AND SMALL SPACES

Inevitably some of the most striking and memorable exotic gardens are those that are on a large scale, where you can wander underneath the leaves of towering palm trees and amongst huge bamboos. These will be the gardens that have the space to display giants such as *Tetrapanax, Gunnera* and great leafy bananas. However even if you only have a small garden, a balcony or just a tiny space within your garden, there is no reason why you can't experiment with exotics.

Many exotics will grow well in pots and this is ideal for a small space or even a balcony, as pot growing inevitably restricts the vigour and keeps plants compact. Hardy exotics, such as specimen *Phormiums*, in pots can be useful for winter colour in key locations, possibly near your house.

Pots are also ideal for new purchases, which are either not big enough to be planted permanently, or for which you don't as yet have the space. Potting them up into larger pots enables them to grow on and for you to enjoy them in the mean time. For example, *Tetrapanax* makes an excellent display plant in a large pot for a couple of years and then can be planted out as a good-sized specimen with immediate impact.

You can try all sorts of exotics in pots, and most will be successful for at least a season. Some of the more vigorous types will require repotting each year, and some will eventually grow to the point where pot culture is too restricted for a large plant.

In some cases, the careful choice of what you grow will enhance their success. For example, with

bananas, choose some of the more compact types such as *Musella lasiocarpa* or *Musa acuminata* 'Zebrina' rather than the very vigorous *Musa basjoo,* which will rapidly show signs of starvation in a pot. Some species may have compact forms, such as *Erythrina crista-gali* which has a form particularly suitable for pot culture. Don't be afraid of growing familiar species in pots. Coleus, *Iresine*, begonias, pelargoniums and other summer bedders provide excellent colour highlights to add to other exotics. A few potted ornamental grasses also provide useful contrasting foliage.

One of the wonderful things about growing exotics in pots is that you can alter and revise the display throughout the season. As plants grow and come into flower, you can move the pots into more prominent positions to better display them. You can re-arrange the mixtures, showing off a plant such as a brilliant white *Agapanthus* first against glossy green *Pittosporum* foliage and then trying it against dark purple banana leaves. Those that grow fast can be moved to the back of a display, and tired plants that

---

HARDY EXOTICS FOR POTS
(can remain outside all year.)

Astelia chathamica 'Silver Spear' or 'Westland'
Cordylines – most types
Lilium – many species and cultivars
Phormium tenax and coloured-leaved cultivars
Tetrapanax papyrifer
Trachycarpus fortunei
Yucca – most types

OPPOSITE PAGE: **Spiky cordylines and palms together with potted specimens in the author's small exotic garden in the Midlands.**

The variegated foliage of *Brugmansia* 'Snowbank' contrasts with the fiery gerbera flowers and vivid purple *Strobilanthes* foliage, but all are grown in pots.

have finished flowering can be thrown away or tucked quietly in a corner. Exotic displays in pots stay dynamic and fresh throughout the season.

You can also use large pots like miniature display beds, by planting a selection of exotics in one container. So for example you might fill a large planter with the tall bronze leaved, orange flowered *Canna* 'Wyoming', complemented by a variegated *Abutilon* 'Souvenir de Bonne'. To this you might add the orange flowered *Dahlia* 'Moonfire', some of the coppery leaved coleus 'Henna' and maybe a spiky feature such as *Cordyline* 'Torbay Dazzler'. Such pots make extremely attractive features in the exotic garden. These display containers are also a great way of trying out a colour scheme on a small scale.

Pots are very practical for exotics that you know will have to be returned to the greenhouse for the winter, such as tender palms, some of the *Agaves*, bromeliads, specimen *Brugmansias* and *Abutilons* and citrus plants. Pot them in good sized pots or planters in a good potting compost, feed well and they will often grow just as well as if planted out.

You can display them as specimens on a paved area, incorporate in a pot display or plunge into a border with other planted exotics. Plunge bedding was an accepted technique for exotics in the nineteenth century, and there is no reason why you cannot revive this technique. Remember that plunged plants will need regular watering, just like any other potted plants.

There are also some excellent terracotta lookalikes made of plastic. These are a good choice for the larger sizes, not only because of cost but when considering weight – not totally hernia-proof but certainly easier to handle. They are unlikely to weather in the same way as clay pots, but they will usually blend in if well planted. They may not be suitable for very large plants however (*see* below).

Glazed pots are often available, but make sure these too are frost resistant and have good drainage holes. Modern aluminium or stainless steel can look great with exotics but tend to be expensive. Containers don't all have to match, but the best effects are created without too much variety. For example terracotta in various shapes and sizes with the odd glazed pot as a highlight can work well.

Citrus have been grown in Europe for centuries, and some of the earliest glasshouses, called orangeries, were built specifically to protect orange trees over winter. Citrus make shapely evergreen bushes, highly suitable for container growing, but they must be moved back under frost-protected glass for the winter. As well as glossy evergreen foliage and the possibility of fruit, citrus have highly scented white flowers. Many garden centres nowadays will offer an extensive range of citrus.

Shopping for Pots

Visit any garden centre, and you will find that the choice of containers is enormous. Many of you may favour classical terracotta pots, available in a wide variety of sizes and shapes. Be sure to get good quality, which is guaranteed to be frost-proof.

This bristly *Yucca rostrata* is displayed in a blue glazed ceramic pot, which contrasts well with the adjacent red brickwork.

Avoid anything twee such as half barrels, pretend cauldrons, willow baskets, look-alike lead urns and other such gimmicks. Having said that, quirky containers can be effective but this is really a matter of personal interest. Probably the best place to search would be a reclamation yard, rather than a garden centre.

When buying a pot, do consider the plant that will go in it. It's important to match the plant and the pot to get the best result. Terracotta suits most plants, but brightly coloured glazed pots will need matching carefully with their occupants. For example a brilliant red glazed pot would be a great contrast to a plant with plain green foliage such as the dwarf palm, *Phoenix roebelenii.*

Growing in Pots

Potted exotics will need a good growing medium to keep them healthy. For large pots or planters, it is usually preferable to use loam-based potting composts, such as John Innes No.3, which will tend to remain stable for a longer period of time than loamless composts.

Because of the restricted root zone, potted exotics will require adequate feeding. You can add a slow-release fertilizer at the potting stage or use a liquid feed regularly throughout the summer months. Adding moisture retaining granules to the potting mix will also reduce the need for watering during dry spells. Cacti and succulents will benefit from compost with additional grit to give good drainage.

All potted exotics will need regular watering. In hot summer weather big leafy plants may need daily watering, making sure you apply enough to thoroughly soak right through the rootzone. Cacti and succulent plants will need a lot less, possibly only weekly watering. For people with a busy lifestyle or who are away from home on occasions, you can buy irrigation kits with timers which will regularly water your pots at set intervals.

Bear in mind that for big specimens, you may need to use a soil-based compost and terracotta pots to give the maximum stability. Although lightweight plastic pots may be preferable for manhandling, when coupled with the lighter loamless composts, big plants such as cannas or bananas will easily catch the wind and blow over.

Never think that growing exotics in pots is second best. The late, great Christopher Lloyd was a fine exponent of pot gardening and this tradition is still continued at his flamboyant Great Dixter garden.

Exotics in Small Spaces

Even if your garden is too small for some of the grand exotics, you can still include some well-chosen hardy exotics such as cordylines, clumping bamboos and maybe a palm or two. In summer, you can add some cannas or other summer colour either in pots or planted out.

When growing in a small space, choose plants that are more compact and have an upright habit. Pruning will also be quite critical, making sure that your exotic plants do not exceed their allocated space or restrict precious sunshine. Most foliage plants such as *Pittosporum, Griselinia* and *Aralia* respond well to careful pruning. Stooled plants such as *Paulownia* are ideal, as they can be kept severely within their place. Herbaceous perennials, such as ornamental grasses are great for small gardens, as they die back each year.

When growing exotics in a small space, always be prepared to take drastic action and remove any plant which is behaving greedily and taking more space than it is worth.

OPPOSITE PAGE: **A small space can be home to a whole host of exotics and create an exciting jungle-like oasis.**

FINAL TOUCHES

Most exotic landscapes are created primarily using a wide range of exotic plants. Great gardens, however, will often include other elements which will add to the overall effect. These may well be traditional landscape materials such as rock, or manmade features such as sculpture, furniture and garden buildings. Inevitably these will need to be specially chosen to enhance our exotic theme. This chapter will explore these final touches.

Exotic Artefacts

The very word sculpture conjures up images of esoteric artwork and immediately sounds elitist, but it can be distinctly fun. Many years ago the Chelsea Flower Show featured an exotic garden by Miles Challis, one of the earliest proponents of the current exotic style. It featured a dark brooding pool, set in a lush background of bananas, from which a huge statue of Poseidon the sea god reared, bearing a menacing trident. Any visit to a good garden centre or flower show will offer you a wide selection of sculpture from classical to crazy. Bear in mind that a bronze bust peaking out from your *Colocassia* or a steel giraffe nibbling on your *Musa basjoo* may sound just perfect, but you will have to be prepared to pay a high price for such artwork. More rustic pieces, such as carved timber, will have a shorter life but would undoubtedly be much cheaper.

OPPOSITE PAGE: **This exotic garden has been created for entertaining, complete with tables, chairs and an outdoor bar underneath rustling palm trees.**

One of the best sources for artefacts to add to your exotic garden is an architectural salvage yard, usually found in most cities. Here you can find almost anything that might have been recovered from demolished houses and cleared gardens. Obvious garden artefacts such as gates, urns, stonework, old chimney pots, ornamental cast iron, seats, statues and edgings are bound to be there. In addition you may find anything from carved stone pillars to a red telephone box. Items for the exotic garden need not be perfect or expensive. Will Giles's exotic garden includes a small stone statue of a slender female, sadly without arms or head. Tucked into a leafy niche, with a skirt of summer foliage, she appears to be demurely hiding behind a green screen.

Occasionally the development of your garden may offer you the ideal opportunity. A tree blown over in a gale can be turned into a sculpture, or a dead standing tree can be painted a bright colour and left as a feature. In a recent London initiative, the plane trees alongside the River Thames were wrapped in red fabric with white spots, giving instant colour and interest. Features need not be elaborate, and such items as terracotta pithoi, glazed pottery and coloured ceramic shapes can be very effective in the right situation.

Furniture

Unless you are one of those gardeners who are never happy unless you're working, you are likely to want places to sit and relax in your exotic garden. This may simply be a secluded seat where you can have a quiet peaceful coffee, or possibly somewhere more extensive, with a table and chairs, for entertaining

An oasis amongst the exotic foliage with a table and chairs, just right for enjoying a quiet coffee on a sunny summer's day.

guests on warm summer evenings. Most gardeners like to spend as much time as possible outdoors, so position such areas where you and your guests have a particularly good view of the garden. Choose garden furniture to fit your garden, whether it be traditional or rather more whimsical. Tim and Tracey's Mediterranean garden in Retford sports a colourful hammock. I have no idea how often it is used in the UK climate, but it's an attractive and whimsical feature, well in style with their relaxing garden. Don't be afraid of colour with garden furniture. A bright red garden seat can be a fabulous feature set against dark green foliage and will look great winter and summer. If you tire of the colour, just get a paint card and choose a new one.

Any garden centre or flower show will offer you a huge range of garden furniture: timber, aluminium, wrought iron or even wicker. Rocking chairs, swings, umbrellas – it's all possible in the exotic garden. Going beyond the standard offerings there are various designers who produce items that are mid way between sculptures and furniture. This creativity will be reflected in the price, but it may be just the unique item you need for a special garden.

Do also consider making your own furniture, adapting store furniture, or searching the second-hand shops. Reclamation yards may yield the remains of old cast iron benches suitable for refurbishment. It's amazing what might be available at a budget price and can be refurbished or adapted for a new use.

Exotic Buildings

If your garden is big enough, you may wish to add a summer house, shelter or garden building of one form or another. Depending on the style of your property, these may be traditional, contemporary or decidedly outrageous. Will Giles's garden includes a Mediterranean loggia in his arid garden, as well as a huge tree house and a charming Victorian summer house complete with thatched roof and leaded light windows. This was dramatically transported by a gang of hefty lads from its original home in the neighbouring garden when the owner got tired of it. Tim and Tracey's garden includes a Mediterranean style cabana, complete with bar for summer entertaining. You will find that tropical style beach huts with thatched roofs are widely available and may be just the thing for a lush jungle garden, or you may wish to design and build something yourself.

Even if you haven't got room for a building you might consider designing a feature wall. Some of you may be lucky enough to have a garden in a wonderful setting with a natural background of trees and the skyline. Others will not be so fortunate and you may have to contend with an ugly fence or blank wall somewhere in your garden. Why not make it part of the display by painting a horticultural backdrop to the exotic theatre you are creating? Maybe paint more bananas or palms to add to those that you have planted or make a desert background for your arid plantings.

A reclaimed sink, some fancy stonework, terracotta pots and exotic plants have made this blank wall into an exciting feature.

Simple low-voltage garden lighting can turn plants like this tender *Dasylirion longissimum* into dynamic night-time features.

Lights and Sound

Many of you may have fallen in love with the magic of tropical gardens, illuminated at night in the warmth of a favourite holiday destination – palm trees festooned with sparkling lights, the stark outlines of spiky foliage lit from below, leafy shadows and the magical twinkle of small glowing bulbs amongst lush foliage. It speaks of hot sultry nights, margaritas, good company and freedom from the cares of the world.

Back home in your own exotic garden, the addition of lighting will contribute another dimension, allowing you to enjoy the garden on dark evenings. Even in winter, you can turn on the outdoor lights and imagine the garden in its full summer glory. Uplighters trained on architectural plants such as palms and spikies will enhance their shapes in stark patterns of light and dark, with dramatic shadows. Rope lights can be used to outline structures or can be wrapped around the trunks of trees. A host of other types of lights can be used in any way you like to add twinkle and glimmer to your landscape. Garden lights are actually very cheap to purchase but, as with all electrical installations in a garden, should be done with care and safety in mind. Some of you may well stay with simple white lights, but of course coloured bulbs give endless possibilities – imagine the fronds of a palm tree outlined in sparkling green lights. And if you have an outdoor dining area, you might add a crystal chandelier.

If you really want to get theatrical, why not add sound to your exotic garden? Many of us will recall that distinct holiday sound of cicadas clicking away in the trees. So you could go the whole way and add a sound track of jungle noises, all the atmosphere of monkeys, exotic bird song, frogs and insects. A quick search on the internet will find you a selection of jungle sounds that can be recorded for looped playback. After all, you are pretending that your exotic garden is an urban jungle. Don't think good taste – just think fun!

DESERT GARDENS

The last really hot, dry, heat-wave summer in the UK was 2006, when the average temperature in Britain was higher than at any time since records began in 1659. Since then summers have been cool and decidedly wet, but despite this a number of exotic gardeners have been bravely experimenting with arid plantings. These plantings of cacti, succulents and other drought loving plants are usually displayed in a rocky, desert style landscape. In Norwich, Will Giles has created an impressive south facing slope, rich with arid plantings; the Old Rectory includes an extensive landscape intended to represent a Californian Wash; and even Christopher Lloyd planted out cacti and succulents on the Lutyens steps by his house. All of these are still exotic gardens, although very different to the lush jungle landscapes described in this book so far.

Real deserts occur in a number of different parts of the world, but they are all characterized by bright sunshine, high temperatures and a lack of water – be it rain, snow, dew or fog. Most deserts will have high daytime temperatures, but because there is no cloud cover the night-time temperatures may plummet. Frost may occur on occasions, and some of the annual precipitation may even be by means of snow. This means that many desert plants may well be frost hardy. Desert style gardens may not be totally realistic, but they will include many plants that grow in desert regions.

OPPOSITE PAGE: **Three tall *Trichocereus*, a smaller hairy *Oreocereus celsianus* and a spiky *Agave mitis* in this desert garden created by Melissa and Keith Scott.**

Desert Plants

Within the plant world there are numerous plants that have natural adaptations to enable them to tolerate dry desert conditions. These are the real survivors which can live through periods of severe water shortage and at the end burst back into healthy growth. Often a plant's leaves are adapted to prevent it from losing excess water in hot dry spells. Cacti and succulent plants are the obvious examples of this. Not only do they have their own store of water within their fleshy leaves and stems, but the surface is often waxy to prevent too much water loss. You can think of them as the camels of the plant kingdom. The presence of silver or blue/grey foliage is also a good indication of a plant's ability to withstand drought. The pale colour reflects the light and reduces the loss of water by transpiration.

Hardy Spikies

Many spiky plants originate from desert areas. Spines are often a plant's protection, preventing it from being eaten by thirsty animals. They are also invariably dramatic plants that add emphasis to most planting schemes. As well as their stark aggressive spiky outlines, many of them have the bonus of dramatic flower spikes. Fortunately many of them are also totally hardy and can be used in the permanent planting within exotic or arid gardens.

Yuccas are good plants to include amongst your desert planting. Most originate from dry desert-like areas of North and Central America. They are in general quite tough, very hardy and tolerant of most conditions, although they do prefer dry well-drained sites. Some types are ground hugging and make a ground level clump with several shoots, but others will make short trunks, like small stocky trees. When in flower, some can be quite spectacular.

One of the best is *Yucca flaccida* 'Ivory', which makes an impressive multi-stemmed plant blooming in the summer with huge towering spikes of ivory white bells. Of the variegated types, probably 'Golden Sword' and 'Bright Edge' are the best, although these are smallish plants and need a spot at the front of the border to be clearly visible. *Yucca rostrata* comes from Mexico and makes an attractive feature plant. On top of its short stocky stem, the silvery foliage is mounted like a large upturned floor mop. Because of its shape,

it is probably best sited as a focal point amongst low growing exotics. The many different types of *Agave* are wonderful spiky desert plants. *Agave americana* is the toughest of all, with blue-green foliage, and can be risked outside as a permanent plant, surviving most winters with minimal protection. There are many others (*see* page 120), although the choicer variegated and tender types will need to be returned to a frost-free greenhouse for the winter.

Members of *Dasylirion, Hesperaloe, Nolina, Beschorneria, Furcraea* and of course *Agave* are all genera which have a similar spiky shape and will fit in well with arid plantings. Most are fairly hardy so can be risked in permanent plantings.

CACTI FOR ARID GARDENS

Paul Spracklin, who gardens in the UK, writes about his experiences growing cacti in coastal Essex, climate zone Z9:

Lots of *Opuntia* are hardy but not many are garden worthy. Most become unattractive invasive weeds, tending to flop over, swamping their neighbours. I would place *O. humifusa* into this category. It is extremely hardy and wet tolerant but simply horrible. *O. cantabrigensis* has a good form with big oval bluish-green pads, and if judiciously

pruned can be kept to a decent framework. It hasn't flowered for me yet, though. One that does flower regularly is *Opuntia rhodacantha*, with smaller spinier pads and lovely lemon yellow flowers that fade to peach after a day or so. A newish one for me, that has very attractive small but dense spines, is *O. sheerei*. It goes without saying that all are horrors to handle, having those nasty little spines.

The uninitiated may be surprised that a few of the large columnar cacti seem quite tough and actually thrive outdoors. I have a spectacular 3.5m (12ft) high *Trichocereus terscheckii* that has grown one third of its height since I planted it out around six years ago. It is possibly the most ridiculously impressive thing I grow. Plus there are numerous others:

Designing Desert Gardens

True deserts are bleak and unfriendly places. All exotic gardens are really horticultural theatre, but they will rarely be realistic. So desert gardens will have elements from reality, somewhat rugged but often glamorized to make them nice and cosy. Most desert gardens are very simple in style, consisting of sweeping undulations with outcrops of rock and widely spaced, striking specimen plants. The main aim should be that it looks good, gives pleasure to the creator and provides a successful environment for growing desert plants.

The floor of your desert garden will probably be composed of sand, or fine gravel, whatever is readily and cheaply available in your area. Check out samples, as some are less attractive than others. It should make a fine pleasing mulch, both ornamental and effective. You can buy aggregates in different sizes for added interest or just use one fine grade which can be raked for a very stark stylized finish.

Rocks are often included in desert landscapes. To be correct, these should ideally be larger pieces derived from the same stone as your surface aggregate. However, for contrast and effect you may opt for something totally different.

Choose some really nice pieces, as big as you can handle – but remember, stone is very heavy and, if not moved with great care, could cause a serious injury.

Trichocereus pasacana, T. escayachensis, T. tarijensis, T. chilensis – all sorts, really.

Echinopsis bruchii and *E. formosa* are a couple of cacti that will eventually grow into barrels. My original plants have grown from satsuma size to watermelon size in a decade, and I now have the most fantastic old mutiheaded specimen that is one of my most prized things. There are many of the smaller species of *Echinopsis* that make small and slowly spreading colonies, such as the common *E. oxygona,* which does well and flowers its head off. Larger snaking colonies are formed by *E. schickendantzii,* which has a mass of colossal flowers that are over in just a night or two.

For flower power try the *Echinocereus,* which are small extremely hardy cacti. My favourites are *E. reichenbachii* in variety, with immense magenta flowers, *E. viridiflorus* with discreet yellow-green flowers and *E. triglochidiatus* that, for me, has yet to flower but forms lovely mats of small cactusy things that are just perfect under larger growing succulents. Also *Chamaecereus sylvestrii,* the peanut cactus is quite hardy, with bright red flowers. One that gets mentioned a lot as bomb-proof hardy is a tiny little alpine cactus from Patagonia – *Maihuenia poepeggii.* To me, when small it looks like a baby hedgehog. After about ten years, it does make a nice dome shaped mat.

These two colourful *Echinopsis* (syn *Soehrensia*) species in Paul Spracklin's garden show that it is possible to successfully grow and flower cacti outdoors in temperate regions.

There are loads more really and all doing the impossible – growing and flowering outside in a damp temperate climate. About as un-English as any garden plants can possibly be!

ABOVE: The arid garden created by Will Giles features many cacti and succulents as well as a small ruined loggia, all on a sunny hillside.

BELOW: Tender succulents, such as this *Agave americana* 'Mediopicta Alba' are best grown in pots so that they can be easily returned to a heated greenhouse for the winter.

Most suppliers will let you choose such pieces yourself, and so it is worth having some idea in advance as to whether you want smooth round boulders, long low pieces or thin slivers that can be installed as upright sentinels.

Generally fewer larger pieces will be far more effective than a greater quantity of small pieces of stone. Remember this is a desert, not a rock garden.

Positioning of stone will often be linked with planting, and as you won't want to be moving stone around a great deal, try to imagine it in its final position or make a sketch to work out the most attractive arrangement.

Always wear leather gloves and boots with steel toe caps when handling large stones. Try to lever or roll rocks, and only lift the smaller pieces. A sack barrow may be useful for moving stones any distance, but be careful that the wheels don't slip into a soft patch and discharge your rocks in totally the wrong place. Planks may be useful for sliding stones into tricky positions.

A good proportion of any stone should always be buried within the ground. This helps the stone to look natural and also gives it stability. Any tall upright stones should be especially well anchored in the ground to avoid them coming loose and being a risk. It may be necessary for big tall stones to be concreted in place to avoid any accidents.

Arranging Desert Plants

The plants that we choose for our desert garden should ideally be large, substantial specimens. This is one garden style where less is definitely more. Big advanced plants are always more expensive, but if you are buying just a few big plants for an area rather than dozens of smaller plants, it is likely that the overall cost may not be much more. Choose your plants carefully, selecting those with good shapes and with a range of heights – low chunky plants, spiky ones and tall thin specimens. Sometimes a less-than-perfect plant with an odd shape may be just the thing to plant alongside a piece of oddly shaped stone. Try to think of the end result in terms of the whole composition.

In a desert garden, the space in between the plants and rocks is as important as the components of the landscape. This will enable you to see the full shape of individual plants or the combined shape of an arrangement of rocks and plants, and often from different angles. These should be a series of small features with clear floorscape between. Such space will also give room for shadows. Bright light casts strong shadows, and these can be a valuable but constantly changing part of the composition.

Cultivating the Desert

Much of the success of cacti and succulents outdoors depends on excellent drainage. When first constructing an arid garden, you should be sure that the soil is thoroughly broken up and mixed with grit, sharp sand or gravel to as much as 50 per cent. Raised beds will also help with drainage, and a sunny location is also essential.

Planting cacti and spiny succulents can be a tricky and sometimes painful business. Always use tough

PLANTS FOR THE DESERT GARDEN

Hardy Desert Plants
Agave americana, A. montana and *A. parryi*
Beschorneria yuccoides and *B. septentrionalis*
Dasylirion wheeleri
Eschscholtzia californica
Hesperaloe parviflora
Yucca – most species
Sempervivum – many species
Sedum – many species
Opuntia robusta, O. catabrigensis and
    O. phaeacantha
Lampranthus – several species, often sold by
    colour

Tender Desert Plants
Aeonium arboreum 'Schwarzkopf'
Agave – most other species and variegated
    types
Aloe arborescens and other spp
Echevaria – many species and cultivars
Furcraea longaeva
Kalanchoe spp
Euphorbias – succulent spp

leather gloves, and handle really prickly subjects by wrapping in thick newspaper. Never plant cacti or succulents deeper than they were in their pots, or the roots will rot. Any tender cacti or succulents should not be planted out until early summer when all danger of frost is past.

Watering will only be necessary in prolonged drought in summer or with pot-grown specimens. Feeding should be moderate to light – no more than two or three times in a summer, with a balanced or low nitrogen fertilizer.

Any plants that are on the borderline of hardiness can be given some overwinter protection mainly from excess rain by sheets of glass fixed above the plants to shed water away from the crown. Some gardeners have developed this idea, creating small temporary greenhouses from timber and plastic sheeting.

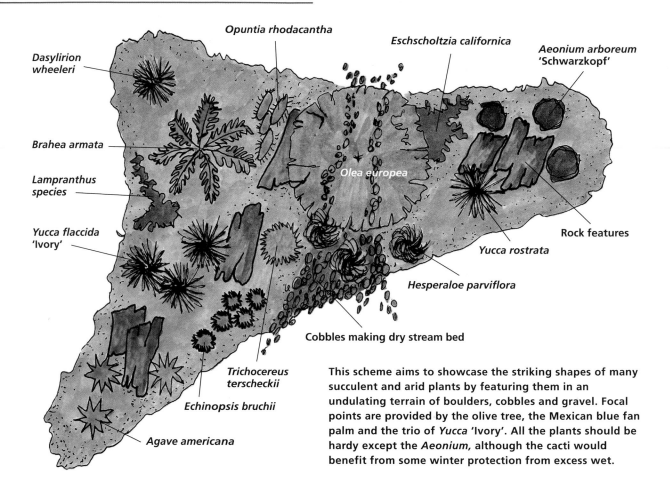

Dasylirion wheeleri

Opuntia rhodacantha

Eschscholtzia californica

Aeonium arboreum 'Schwarzkopf'

Brahea armata

Olea europea

Lampranthus species

Rock features

Yucca flaccida 'Ivory'

Yucca rostrata

Hesperaloe parviflora

Cobbles making dry stream bed

Trichocereus terscheckii

Echinopsis bruchii

Agave americana

This scheme aims to showcase the striking shapes of many succulent and arid plants by featuring them in an undulating terrain of boulders, cobbles and gravel. Focal points are provided by the olive tree, the Mexican blue fan palm and the trio of *Yucca* 'Ivory'. All the plants should be hardy except the *Aeonium*, although the cacti would benefit from some winter protection from excess wet.

This whimsical 'undersea' garden in California features many fascinating cacti and succulents, including *Aloe vanbalenii*, the octopus aloe.

The desert wash at East Ruston Old Vicarage, filled with spiky foliage and bright colour from *Eschscholtzia*, *Zauschneria* and *Verbena bonariense*.

Desert Wash

The innovative East Ruston Old Vicarage contains an arid garden designed to resemble a desert wash. Washes are dry creeks, usually at the base of mountains, that channel water after storms. They may be natural or sometimes man-made but will usually contain boulders and stones washed down by storm surges. The extra moisture that these desert areas receive means that they often support a wide range of plants.

The wash at East Ruston consists of a series of rocky gouges through the landscape, dotted with flints and boulders and bisected by pathways and wooden bridges. This extensive garden is full of spiky plants such as yucca, aloes, puyas, agaves, beschorneria and dasylirion. Colour is provided by blue agapanthus and orange eschscholtzia, which seed freely throughout the area. The excellent drainage created in this garden means that various succulents and cacti remain dry at the roots and are able to tolerate the cold, creating the impossibility of an Arizona desert wash in chilly East Anglia.

UNDER THE SEA
'I'd like to be, under the sea, in an octopus's garden, in the shade'

The lyrics of this classic Beatles' song are no doubt better known than a unique 'undersea' garden in California designed by San Diego Botanical Garden staff. This whimsical landscape utilizes a host of ironically drought-resistant plants and stone to mimic an underwater seascape. Specimens of the sinuous *Aloe vanbalenii*, the octopus aloe, feature along with other succulents. *Euphorbia tirucalli* 'Sticks on Fire' glows beautifully in cooler weather, in lovely coral red tints. Volcanic stone, fossils, shells, an anchor, a turtle sculpture and other maritime bric-a-brac all contribute to this fascinating theatrical garden.

Although this is a warm climate garden, there is no reason why you can't take inspiration from this and recreate something like it using hardy succulents such as sedums and sempervivums, together with grasses and other foliage plants to give the swirl of seaweed. The twisted leaves of *Juncus effusus* 'Spiralis' can easily convince you it might grow underwater! A trip to the coast to collect some driftwood, shells and beach combings, and you have the makings of your own octopus's garden.

A–Z OF EXOTIC PLANTS

Hardiness Ratings

It is very difficult to be precise about the subject of hardiness. A particularly desirable exotic plant may be hardy in one garden but may die over winter in a nearby garden, even if tried repeatedly. This can be due to any number of local factors, such as microclimate, aspect, soil, drainage or shelter. So any recommendations can only be generalizations.

At the beginning of each entry you will find a broad comment on hardiness, based on the Royal Horticultural Society hardiness ratings and largely relevant to the UK.

After most individual plant listings there is a Z symbol with a number, referring to a hardiness system developed in the USA based on annual minimum temperatures for certain areas or zones. This system is now being recognized and used outside the USA, and I have used it here. Plants are rated with the lowest zone in which they are likely to survive over winter. So if a plant is listed as a Z8 plant it is likely also to survive in the warmer Zone 9 but not the cooler Zone 7 or lower. In the summer months plants will nevertheless grow outside in a lower zone, providing they are given winter frost protection. So for example, a Z11 plant can be bedded out for the summer in Zone 8.

The UK is a small island and does not have great differences of climate, so generally experiences conditions between Zones 7 and 9. The majority of the country is Zone 8, with the north of Scotland in Zone 7, whereas the south west, parts of southern Ireland and other coastal areas are Zone 9. Much of Europe spans Zones 7 to 10.

I have given hardiness ratings for each plant where possible, based not only on published documentation but also on my own experiences and those of others who dabble with exotics, so you may find some surprising listings.

The 'Totally Hardy' plants should survive any location and be winter hardy outdoors in temperate areas. 'Generally Hardy' plants are also tough and should survive most areas and all but extreme winters. Plants listed as 'Borderline Hardy' are the gambles and may or may not survive a temperate winter depending on your local conditions. The 'Half Hardy' plants will tolerate no frost, so require winter protection, usually in a heated glasshouse, which will vary in the temperature required (*see* each plant entry).

Award of Garden Merit

Plants designated as AGM have been awarded this standard by the Royal Horticultural Society, often following competitive trials at one of their gardens. Such plants must have achieved outstanding garden performance, be easy to grow, resistant to pest and disease and be readily available in the nursery trade.

OPPOSITE PAGE: **Amongst the vast range of exotic plants, there are lots with beautiful flowers, but particularly many with striking coloured foliage.**

GUIDE TO HARDINESS RATINGS			
Totally Hardy	RHS **H4**,	Zone 7	Tolerates –18°C to –12°C (0 to 10°F)
Generally Hardy	RHS **H3–4**	Zone 8	Tolerates –12°C to –7°C (10 to 20°F)
Borderline Hardy	RHS **H3**	Zone 9	Tolerates –7°C to –1°C (20 to 30°F)
Half Hardy	RHS **H1+3**	Zone 10	Summer outside, winter heated glass

Abutilon

Malvaceae

Generally Hardy and Half Hardy

A genus of fast growing sun loving shrubby perennials, many of which come from South America. *Abutilon vitifolium* and the hybrid *A. x* 'Suntense' are suitable for permanent planting, and both produce blue saucer-like flowers in early summer. Both grow to 3m (10ft) or more. *A. vitifolium* 'Tennant's White' AGM is white and slightly less hardy. *A. megapotanicum* AGM grows to 90cm (3ft) producing very wiry growths and small bell-shaped red and yellow flowers throughout the season. There is also a variegated form, and both are best trained against a wall or used as trailers in a container. 'Kentish Belle' and 'Patrick Synge' are also tough and easy to grow, making great wall shrubs. All these are Z8.

There are also a whole host of half hardy cultivars (Z10) with open bell shaped flowers in a wide range of colours, that are not frost hardy so must be overwintered under glass and planted out for summer display only. Most make about 1.5m (5ft) in a season. 'Canary Bird' AGM has bright yellow flowers, 'Nabob' AGM is deep red, and 'Boule de Neige' is white. *A. pictum* 'Thompsonii' is a very familiar golden variegated cultivar with orange flowers, somewhat taller than 'Cannington Peter' AGM, which is also variegated but with red flowers. 'Souvenir de Bonne' AGM is a tall growing cultivar with white edges to green leaves and bright orange flowers. Don't confuse with 'Savitzei' AGM, which is a lovely compact cultivar with a lot of white in its leaves and dusky brown flowers.

Abutilons prefer full sun and a moist fertile soil. All propagated by semi-ripe cuttings taken in the autumn and overwintered under frost-free glass, about 10°C (50°F). There is also a seed raised range called the 'Bella series' which, although free flowering and colourful, do not really grow tall enough to be effective in an exotic garden.

Acacia

Leguminosae

Borderline Hardy

Evergreen shrubs and trees, mainly from Australia, a few of which are hardy enough for temperate areas.

Abutilon 'Kentish Belle' is virtually hardy when grown against a warm wall and flowers continuously throughout the summer months.

They are mostly drought tolerant, requiring full sun and a well drained soil. *A. dealbata* AGM (Z9) and *A. baileyana* AGM (Z10) are both fast growing, making small trees with very delicate finely cut silvery green foliage and clusters of lemon yellow flowers, which most people will recognize as the cut flower sold in florists as mimosa. They will reach at least 5m (16ft). You may also find *A. pravissima* AGM (Z10), which is best grown against a wall, with curious wedge shaped foliage, and yellow flowers. Hardy and reasonably successful in a sunny sheltered site.

Acanthus

Acanthaceae

Totally Hardy

These are hardy herbaceous perennials grown mainly for their handsome glossy green foliage. They will grow almost anywhere in either sun or shade and so can be used as filler plants under taller species such as bamboo. They do flower in midsummer with spikes of unusual funnel-shaped white and mauve flowers, but their main value is their foliage. *A. mollis* (Z7) is the most familiar, but *A. spinosus* AGM (Z7) has the more finely cut and attractive foliage. They grow to just over 1m (4ft). Both are semi-evergreen and resent disturbance, so should be planted and left alone. Propagate by division.

Aeonium

Crassulaceae

Half Hardy

This is a group of elegant succulents grown for their foliage. They are not frost hardy, so need to be overwintered under heated glass and brought out for summer display. They can be planted out in a sunny well-drained location or left in their pots. *A. arboreum* AGM (Z10) is quite familiar, most often seen as the

This wonderful purple-leaved *Aeonium*, sold as 'Atropurpureum' or often 'Schwarzkopf', looks good contrasted with this variegated *Miscanthus*.

purple leaved form 'Atropurpureum' AGM (syn 'Schwarzkopf'). It makes a small rugged bush, around 45cm (18in) high, covered in rich almost black rosettes of glossy foliage. There is also a variegated type called 'Sunburst '.There are many other aeoniums such as *A. balsamiferum* (Z10) which has rosettes of silvery foliage and makes a small shrubby plant and *A. tabuliforme* AGM (Z10) which makes huge flat rosettes of overlapping leaves – quite spectacular. *A. simsii* (Z8) seems to be the only reliably hardy species. Grow in a well drained sandy compost to ensure that plants are well anchored. Propagate by means of offsets, which are rooted like cuttings.

Agapanthus

Agapanthaceae/Liliaceae

Borderline Hardy

The *Agapanthus* are clump forming perennials, originating in South Africa and including both hardy and tender species. In general they have narrow strap-like green leaves which may be evergreen or die back in the winter. In general the evergreen species are tender and the deciduous types hardy. They mostly grow to around 60cm (2ft) and produce large heads of small tubular flowers which are generally blue or sometimes white. All revel in hot sunny locations, and although they prefer a moist site, they will tolerate quite dry conditions. Flowering is most prolific when plants are left undisturbed. *A. africanus* (Z8) and *A. praecox* (Z9) and their hybrids are evergreen types, whilst *A. inapertus* (Z7) is an example of a deciduous type. There are many different named cultivars available. Agapanthus make excellent subjects for large pots or tubs. This is undoubtedly the best way to grow the more tender types, as they can easily be moved back under glass for the winter. Propagation is by division.

Agave

Agavaceae

Generally Hardy to Half Hardy

These succulent plants originate from Central and Southern America. In general they make spiky plants with sword-shaped leaves that are often very sharply toothed or armed with vicious needle-like points. These can be seriously dangerous, especially to children.

The commonest of all is *Agave americana* AGM (Z8), the century plant, which makes a tough evergreen specimen. Given time it will make a magnificent feature, as much as 2m (6ft) tall. Under temperate conditions, it will usually survive from year to year outside, given a sheltered location; however the battering of rain and wind usually means that such plants often look a little shabby. The similar *A. salmiana* (Z9) and *A. mitis* (Z9) also occur in mild sheltered gardens. Hardy clones of these exist but it's somewhat of a gamble obtaining them. Enthusiasts may like to search out *A. montana* (Z8), which is hardy and has huge garden potential. *Agave gentryi* 'Jaws' (Z8) and *A. parrasana* (Z8) are other hardy ones worth tracking down. Some gardeners have also had success with *A. tequilana* (Z9), the source of tequila!

The variegated forms, such as *A. americana* 'Striata' (Z10) which has gold striped leaves or 'Mediopicta' AGM (Z10) with a bold white band down the centre of the leaves, are both tender and must return to the greenhouse each winter. The tender *Agave desmettiana* (Z10) is particularly curvaceous, with arched leaves giving the whole plant a graceful vase shape.

Flowering of agaves is occasional but quite spectacular when it happens, with huge towering spikes that may reach to 5m (17ft) or more. Although the individual flowers are unimpressive, the sheer scale of the spike is quite spectacular. After flowering the main spike dies, but side shoots are produced which continue the growth pattern.

They all need full sun and a very well-drained poor soil, so are excellent plants for the arid garden. All of them can be propagated by offsets, which are produced around the base of the main plant. Some produce bulbils on the flowering stems.

Alocasia

Araceae

Half Hardy

These lush foliage plants come from the tropical rainforests of South Asia. They are sometimes called 'upright elephant's ears' to distinguish from *Colocasia*. Leaves are usually large, shield-shaped, upward pointing and may be attractively marked. *Alocasia macrorrhiza* (Z10), the giant taro, is an impressive foliage plant bearing broad, glossy green, heart-shaped leaves held on long slender stems. Flower is a yellowish green spathe. Although not the most spectacular, this is probably the easiest to obtain. Also *A.* x 'Portora' (Z10) (formerly known as 'Portadora') which is a hybrid cross of *A. odora* and *A. portei.* This makes a stunning architectural specimen with giant, green, heavily scalloped leaves, growing to as much as 1.5m (5ft). Some gardeners have had success with *A.* 'Calidora' (Z10), the giant elephant's ear. Both seem to do well in temperate climates. These grow from fleshy rootstocks which must be overwintered under cover and divided in the spring. Some gardeners keep them growing at a minimum of 5°C (40°F) with minimum water, which gives a head-start on next year.

A. sanderiana (Z11) has dark black-green, arrow-shaped leaves with a metallic sheen, conspicuously marked with silver veins. Likely to be found amongst houseplants at a garden centre, but worth trying outside.

Aloe arborescens **needs a very warm, sunny, well-drained location or should be returned to a frost-free greenhouse for the winter.**

Aloe

Aloeaceae/Liliaceae

Borderline Hardy

A group of many evergreen succulents, originating from many areas of Africa and suitable for arid borders. Similar in appearance to agaves. Many aloes make low level rosettes of spiky foliage, although some make shrubs or small trees. *A. ferox* (Z9) is frost hardy and makes a stocky, shrubby plant around 1.5m (5ft), with spiny grey foliage and spikes of red tubular flowers on mature plants. If you want yellow flowers, try *A. striatula* (Z9), which is frost hardy. *Aloe arborescens* (Z9) makes a small tree-like plant, up to 2m (6ft) with orange-red flowers. It should go back under glass for the winter, to be cautious. Grow all of these in a very well drained soil and sunny location. Propagate by rooting offsets as cuttings.

Alternanthera

Amaranthaceae

Half Hardy

A genus of brilliantly coloured but tender foliage plants, often used for carpet bedding so mostly too insubstantial for the exotic garden. The most suitable is the vividly coloured *Alternanthera dentata* 'Purple Knight' (Z11), grown from seed or plugs, which makes a carpet of vibrant almost black foliage, about 30cm (12in) tall. Grow as a seasonal plant and throw away in the autumn.

Amicia

Fabaceae

Borderline Hardy

The species generally available is *Amicia zygomeris* (Z9), a curious herbaceous perennial producing leaves with four leaflets, rather like green butterflies with conspicuous red stipules. It grows to just over 1m (4ft) and in late summer produces yellow pea-like flowers. Grow in full sun and propagate by seed or basal cuttings.

Amorphophallus

Araceae

Half Hardy

This is a genus of bizarre plants, sometimes highlighted by the titan lily, which is probably the world's biggest and worst smelling flower. It blooms only a few times in its 40-year life span. Its foul smelling, deep purple flower can be up to 3m (10ft) across and almost as tall. Because it is a native of the Borneo rain forest, it is rarely seen except in botanic gardens, where its rare blooming always causes a sensation.

The related *Amorphophallus konjac* (Z7) is sometimes offered for sale and is worth growing for its exotic foliage alone. The single but much divided leaf can grow up to 2m (7ft) looking like a small tree. It produces a foul smelling purple spathe. Growth is from a swollen tuberous root, which can be planted permanently and mulched, but it is better started off in a warm greenhouse and planted outside for the summer. The trick is to remove the small offsets each year, encouraging all the growth into one monster leaf.

Aralia

Araliaceae

Totally Hardy

These dramatic woody plants make striking shrubs or small trees, reaching to 3m (10ft) or more. *Aralia elata* AGM (Z4), the Japanese angelica tree, produces tough stems covered with sharp spines topped with large head of finely cut green foliage. Suckers freely,

forming a small thicket of similar stems with foliage at different heights. There are also a couple of classy variegated types, *A. elata* 'Variegata' AGM (Z4), which has creamy white foliage, and the more sophisticated golden 'Aureovariegata' (Z4). Both grow to just under 2m (6ft). They make striking permanent specimen plants with huge showy leaves, so position them in key locations. Fairly tolerant but prefer moist fertile soils and sunny locations for strongest leaf colourings with variegated types. Both of these are propagated by grafting so are extremely expensive to buy.

Astelia

Liliaceae

Generally Hardy

This is a group of clump-forming evergreen perennials with spiky foliage. They are gaining a reputation for being very tolerant of different conditions and are virtually hardy. The most commonly available cultivar is the silvery *Astelia chathamica* AGM (Z8), often sold as 'Silver Spear'. The closely related *A. nervosa* 'Westland' (Z9) has coppery bronze foliage and seems to be just as easy and tolerant. Both grow to about 60cm (2ft). They prefer a sunny, sheltered and moist location. Propagation is by division, although gardeners report that establishing new divisions is difficult.

Begonia

Begoniaceae

Half Hardy

Well-known for the big blowsy blooms produced from the tuberous types, which can well be used in the exotic garden. The foliage houseplants such as *Begonia rex* (Z11) and its many cultivars can equally be used outside for summer display, providing they are hardened off carefully and given a shady location.

Position *Begonia grandis* subsp *evansiana* where it will catch the sunshine to highlight the rich red veins on the underside of the leaves.

In particular, *B. grandis* subsp *evansiana* AGM (Z6) is worth including in the exotic garden. This lush green-leaved foliage plant is hardy enough to stay outside all the year round, although it dies down to the ground each winter. The undersides of the leaves are a rich bronze and glow in bright sunshine. It will make 45cm (18in) growth with small pink flowers. Grow in moist soil in partial shade.

Bergenia

Saxifragaceae

Totally Hardy

These are useful evergreen groundcover plants that will tolerate almost any situation, although they prefer moist shade. Most have large oval-shaped, glossy green leaves and hug the ground, growing to no more than 30cm (12in), even when flowering. The pink or white flowers produced in spring are really irrelevant to the exotic garden. Use bergenias as groundcover under other hardy exotics such as bamboo. There are many cultivars, of which

'Ballawley' AGM (Z4) has good sized leaves and *B. cordata* 'Tubby Andrews' (Z4) is variegated. The choicest of them all is *B. ciliata* (Z5), a species from the Himalayas with gigantic hairy leaves. Not quite as tough as the others but a 'must have' for a sheltered location. Propagate by division.

Beschorneria

Agavaceae

Generally and Borderline Hardy

These spiky-leaved plants can easily be mistaken for silvery-looking yuccas or even agaves, but when in flower are quite distinct. *Beschorneria septentrionalis* (Z8) produces an arching red stem, around 1.5m (5ft) tall, topped with trailing maroon and green flowers. For an even more impressive display, try *B. yuccoides* AGM (Z9), which is similar but grows to 3m (10ft) or more. Be sure to grow them well back from the edge of borders or the curving stems tend to block pathways. Ideally plant a group on a bank, where the sumptuous flowers will appear to flow down the slope.

Bidens

Asteraceae/Compositae

Half Hardy

This genus contains many species of small yellow or white flowered daisies. It is included amongst exotics because of the prolific nature of its flowering and speed of growth. The common species *Bidens ferulifolia* AGM (Z9) is a vigorous trailing or spreading plant with finely cut green foliage and masses of small yellow daisies from planting until the frosts. In a single season a small plant can make a carpet of yellow flowers, well over 1m (4ft) in diameter, but no more than 15cm (6in) tall. New cultivars include 'Peter's Gold Carpet', 'Peter's Gold Rush', 'Peter's Surprise' and 'Sun Kiss', all of which have larger flowers and a tighter habit of growth. You will find them in garden centres amongst patio and basket plants in early summer. They are useful as carpeting plants under taller exotics.

Bougainvillea

Nyctaginaceae

Half Hardy

These colourful tropical climbers seem to epitomize holiday locations with their neon bright flowers prolifically produced in so many colours. In fact the flowers themselves are small and insignificant, but it is the brilliantly coloured bracts that surround the flower that are particularly showy. Sadly they are truly tropical and do not thrive in temperate climates. They can be grown in glass houses and brought outside for summer display, although pot grown specimens never seem to have the abundance of flower that one would like. Specialist nurseries offer numerous cultivars. In particular *B. x buttiana* 'Raspberry Ice' (Z10) is worth growing, as it has variegated foliage as well as pink bracts.

Brahea

Arecaceae

Borderline Hardy

The most familiar species is *Brahea armata* (Z9), the Mexican blue palm, which is a choice and highly desirable plant. This palm has extremely attractive blue-grey foliage in huge lustrous fans. It actually originates from California, and although it is virtually frost hardy it still needs a very warm and sheltered location to grow well. It is well worth trying, as a healthy mature plant is quite spectacular and probably the bluest of all palms. Under temperate conditions it is unlikely to exceed 2m (7ft). Plant in a well-drained but moist soil and give winter protection with a screen of loosely wrapped fleece or hessian whilst young.

Brugmansia

Solanaceae

Half Hardy

This is a genus of shrubby perennials with spectacular trumpet shaped flowers that are often intoxicatingly scented. Coming from South America, they are mostly tender and so will require overwintering under frost-free conditions but are fast growing and respond well to heavy feeding. These plants are most effective when tall enough that you can look up into the trumpets, so it is worthwhile keeping plants from year to year.

The species *Brugmansia sanguinea* (Z9) has large yellow and red tubular flowers and is virtually hardy. On occasions, it can survive outside against a dry sheltered wall for years. There are many other named cultivars mainly in pastel shades. *B. x candida* 'Grand Marnier' AGM (Z10) is a good soft apricot, and the species *B. arborea* 'Knightii' AGM (Z10) has frilly, snowy white flowers which are strongly fragrant. There are also variegated types such 'Maya' (Z10) (syn 'Sunset') and the newer and spectacular 'Snowbank' also with apricot flowers fading to white. Most will

This *Brugmansia* 'Grand Marnier' is best appreciated as an older larger plant, when the flowers are displayed at eye level or above.

grow to just under 2m (6ft) in a season. Specialist collectors, particularly in America and Germany, have been introducing some wonderful new cultivars in recent years. A word of warning – all brugmansias are highly poisonous and should be treated with care, always washing your hands after handling. They are easy to propagate from softwood or hardwood cuttings but must be overwintered in a frost-free greenhouse at about 8°C (45°F) or ideally warmer. They are particularly prone to attack by whitefly and red spider mite.

Butia

Arecaceae/Palmae

Borderline Hardy

Known mainly for *Butia capitata* (Z9), the jelly palm.

The fruits from mature plants are used to make jam, known of course as jelly in the USA. This is a feather palm, with long arching, almost curled leaf stems, clothed with narrow green or blue-grey leaflets. The variability is likely to be due to hybridization with other species in this genus. Makes a good specimen palm but is slow growing and unlikely to exceed 2m (7ft) in temperate climates. Plant in full sun in a well-drained soil.

Caladium

Araceae

Half Hardy

These exquisite plants are truly tropical and very demanding even for the experienced gardener. Often sold as angel's wings, they grow from fleshy tubers

Despite originating in Australia, *Callistemon rigidus* is totally hardy and will flower reliably and freely, early each summer.

and produce slender stems topped with dancing, heart-shaped leaves, brilliantly marked in vivid shades of red, white and pink. Grows to about 45cm (18in). Have a go at growing them when you want something really challenging but potentially dazzling!

Grow them in a humid greenhouse, heated to at least 16°C (60°F). In midsummer you can play the gamble of displaying them outside in a very warm sheltered location for a few weeks. By growing in pots and just using them as seasonal colour, you can rapidly take them back to the protective environment of a greenhouse if the summer turns nasty.

Callistemon

Myrtaceae

Generally Hardy

The bottlebrush plants are grown for their cylindrical flower spikes made up of numerous tiny thread-like flowers, commonly in red. Most of these are evergreen shrubs originating from Australia, making narrow upright plants with small emerald green leaves. One of the best red ones is *Callistemon citrinus* 'Splendens' AGM (Z8), which is tough and hardy. A well-grown plant will reach 1.5m (5ft) and will be covered with red flowers in midsummer. You may also like to try *C. pallidus* (Z8), which is similar but produces pale lemon yellow flowers. Grow in full sun in a sheltered location. Propagate by cuttings in autumn.

Campsis

Bignoniaceae

Generally Hardy

These are the trumpet creepers, a series of woody climbers that seem to be confused botanically with the very similar genus *Tecoma,* which is widely grown in warmer climates. *Campsis x tagliabuana* 'Madame Galen' AGM (Z8) is the most readily available. This is a slow-growing climber with pinnate foliage, which ultimately produces large clusters of vivid, soft red trumpets. Eventually makes about 2.75m (9ft). Plant it in a warm sheltered location and feed generously to encourage growth.

Canna

Cannaceae

Half Hardy

These tropical foliage and flowering plants, originating from South America have been well described in Chapter 5. The lush foliage is produced from a fleshy rhizome that is used to overwinter the plant in temperate climates. They are greedy plants and respond well to a warm sunny location, rich soils, generous feeding and watering. The foliage is tender and quickly browns with even the slightest frost. Overwinter by digging up the rhizomes and storing in frost-free conditions. These are then divided in the spring and started into fresh growth in a warm greenhouse at around 10°C (50°F) or warmer. Many gardeners have also had success by leaving the rhizomes in the soil and covering with a thick but loose mulch. When grown in this way, flowering may be a little later, and eventually the clumps will become congested and need dividing. Mostly Z8 but usually treated as half hardy. There are many excellent old and new cultivars.

Canna Virus

In recent years, cannas have been increasingly decimated by various virus diseases, which cause distorted, mottled foliage, stunting and deformed flowers. Sadly, once infected there is no cure, and you must destroy all plants showing symptoms before the virus spreads. Many gardeners and even nurseries have not recognized the seriousness of these diseases, and because of this there are many infected stocks being distributed. To avoid virus, never purchase the dry rhizomes, which may be diseased as the virus cannot be seen at this stage. Only buy growing plants, which can be inspected for healthy growth, with well coloured foliage, free of spots and stunting. Despite this problem, cannas are still well worth while growing.

Cannas *en masse* produce a kaleidoscope of exotic colour throughout the summer months until the first frosts of autumn.

CANNAS FOR FLOWERS			
Name	Height	Foliage	Flowers
'Assaut'	2m (6ft)	Purple	Large maroon
'Australia'	2m (6ft)	Rich bronze	Large orange
'Black Knight'	2m (6ft)	Deep purple	Large dark red
'Cleopatra'	1m (4ft)	Green/purple	Yellow-red
'En Avant'	1m (4ft)	Green	Yellow + red spots
C. iridiflora 'Ehemannii' AGM	2m (6ft)	Green foliage	Pendant cerise
'King Humbert'	2m (6ft)	Bronze	Large blood red
'Louis Cayeux' AGM	90cm (3ft)	Green	Salmon pink
'Lucifer'	50cm (2ft)	Green	Red and yellow
'Panache'	1.5m (5ft)	Green	Small pale apricot
'President'	1.5m (5ft)	Green	Scarlet
'Richard Wallace'	1m (4ft)	Green	Large yellow
'Rosemond Coles'	1.5m (5ft)	Green	Red and yellow
'Wyoming' AGM	2m (6ft)	Bronze	Large orange

CANNAS FOR FOLIAGE

'Phasion' AGM (syn 'Durban')	1.5m (5ft)	Purple multicoloured	Large orange
C. indica 'Purpurea'	2m (6ft)	Bronze	Small orange
C. musifolia 'Grande'	2m (6ft)	Huge green leaves	Insignificant
'Mystique' AGM	2m (6ft)	Purple iridescent	Small, vivid red
'Striata' AGM (syn 'Praetoria')	1.5m (5ft)	Yellow variegated	Large orange

The rich foliage of *Canna* 'Durban', sometimes sold as 'Phasion', makes it worth growing for its leaves alone, but it does also have bright orange flowers.

Catalpa

Bignoniaceae

Totally Hardy

This genus contains the Indian bean trees, mainly from North America. *Catalpa bignonioides* AGM (Z5) is the most familiar, with large green leaves and prettily marked white flowers in midsummer. The long green seed pods lead to the common name but are not edible. If left to grow freely, it makes an impressive spreading tree up to 10m (30ft). The golden-leaved cultivar *C. b.* 'Aurea' AGM (Z5) is less vigorous. The somewhat slower growing *C. x erubescens* 'Purpurea' AGM (Z5) has lovely iridescent purple foliage when the growth is young. In the exotic garden, these are often stooled to encourage even larger leaves (*see* page 24) on a more compact plant.

Cautleya

Zingiberaceae

Generally Hardy

Cautleya spicata (Z8) is a tough perennial ginger from China, with lush dagger-shaped leaves and slender red flower stems, bearing curious yellow flowers in midsummer. An easy plant with a distinctly exotic look. Grows to about 90cm (3ft). Mulch the roots in autumn to protect overwinter. Propagate by division in spring.

Catalpa bignoniodes 'Aurea', the golden form of the Indian bean tree can be pruned hard each spring to get vigorous foliage like this.

Centaurea

Compositae

Generally Hardy

Included for the silver-leaved types, known as dusty millers. There are various seed raised types, but the best is *Centaurea gymnocarpa* (Z8), which makes wonderful cushions of floppy, finely divided silver foliage. Grows to about 50cm (18in). Botanically this may now be classified as a *Cineraria* or even *Senecio*. Makes an excellent contrast to bright colours. Root from heeled cuttings in the autumn and overwinter under cool glass, 5°C (40°F). Prefers a sunny well-drained site but very tolerant.

Cercis

Leguminosae/Papilionaceae

Totally Hardy

Included here for the sumptuous *Cercis canadensis* 'Forest Pansy' AGM (Z4), which makes a substantial shrub or small tree, 3m (10ft) or more in height. The large heart-shaped leaves in rich wine red look particularly stunning when the light shines through the foliage. It responds well to hard spring pruning resulting in especially lush leaves.

Chamaerops

Arecaceae/Palmae

Generally Hardy

The Mediterranean fan palm, *Chamaerops humilis* AGM (Z8), is the best known member of this genus. This is a compact, multi-stemmed palm making a short bushy plant around 2m (6ft) with wiry and prickly green fans of foliage. It is tough and hardy, but slow growing. The form 'Cerifera' (syn var. *argentea*) is as blue as the Mexican blue palm but much hardier and still has the compact habit of the species. They make good pot plants when young or can be planted out in a well-drained location.

Chlorophyttum

Liliaceae

Half Hardy

This is the much maligned and often neglected windowsill resident, the spider plant. As a grassy foliage plant it makes good exotic groundcover under taller species and is an effective contrast to broader-leaved plants. The common one is *C. comosum* 'Variegatum' (Z10) with green strap leaves margined with cream, growing to about 25cm (9in). A recent

Small citrus trees are often available in garden centres, complete with fruit, but must be overwintered in a frost-free greenhouse.

They make excellent evergreen bushes in a container, with sweetly perfumed white flowers and if you are lucky, fruit. They are tender so need to spend the winter under heated glass, ideally 10°C (50°F) or warmer but are quite happy outside as feature plants in summer. Water and feed carefully, and they will last many years. Some intrepid growers report overwintering them outdoors in the UK but without fruit. If you want fruit, do buy a named cultivar such as the lemon *Citrus x meyeri* 'Meyer' AGM (Z10) rather than just growing pips, which will not breed true to type. The bizarrely shaped *Citrus medica* var. *digitata*, also called Buddha's Hand, is shaped like a chunky yellow octopus. You may also find a few, such as the dwarf calamondin, in local garden centres.

cultivar called 'Ocean' is superior, making compact bushy plants. Propagate by rooting offsets and overwintering at around 10°C (50°F).

Citrus

Rutaceae

Half Hardy

This genus embraces the whole host of fruiting citrus including oranges, lemons, grapefruits and limes.

Cobaea

Polemoniaceae

Half Hardy

Although technically perennial climbers, these are normally grown as annuals from seed each year, but they may survive in mild winters. Originating from South America, they are fast growing and climb by tendrils to 2.75m (9ft) or more. Commonly known as the cup and saucer vine, *Cobaea scandens* AGM (Z11) has flowers made up of large blue bells sitting on a prominent calyx. There is also an excellent greenish white variety *C. scandens* f. *alba* AGM, well worth growing. Sow seed in a warm greenhouse in spring and grow in a moist, fertile soil.

Colocasia

Araceae

Half Hardy

These are also called elephant's ears and should not to be confused with *Alocasia*. These are tender tuberous perennials from tropical Asia, producing exotic arrow-shaped leaves, some with prominent veins. Flowers are rarely produced and tend to be insignificant small white spathes. Although widely grown as a staple food in some countries, the tubers are poisonous and an irritant if ingested without cooking. The sap can also be an irritant.

Colocasia esculenta AGM (Z10) is the basic commercial taro, producing lush green leaves, and these can be obtained from supermarkets and often coaxed into growth at a fraction of the price of those bought from nurseries. Grows to around 90cm (3ft) However there are some excellent cultivars such as 'Mammoth' and 'Jack's Giant', both with colossal green leaves or the tough *C. esculenta* 'Fontanesii', with dark red to purple stalks. 'Black Magic' is a very choice form of this plant with huge inky black leaves. This is quite stupendous but very tender, so tends not to perform to its maximum in cool areas. Still well worth trying. The tubers should be started under heated glass at a minimum of 18°C (64°F) and planted out after all danger of frost is past. Outdoors, select a warm, sheltered area with moist soil and light shade. Some gardeners have had success with mulching the roots in autumn and leaving in situ, but to be sure, tubers should be lifted and kept dry and frost-free overwinter.

Cordyline

Agavaceae

Generally Hardy

These are the cabbage palms, mainly forms of *Cordyline australis* AGM (Z8), originating in New Zealand. All are spiky shrubs and eventually small trees with narrow linear foliage, radiating from a central stem. Initially young plants have a single growing point and rosette of foliage, but older plants that have flowered or suffered damage will develop into branched specimens that can be extremely attractive. The basic species is green, and there is a bronze version called 'Atropurpurea' (Z8), both of which are generally hardy in temperate areas and will develop

into sizeable small trees, 4m (13ft) or more tall. They will ultimately flower with sickly sweet white flowers. In addition there are many fancy coloured leaf versions that are less hardy, mainly Z9 and best moved under cold glass for the winter. 'Torbay Dazzler' AGM has variegated foliage; 'Purple Tower' AGM, deep wine coloured leaves; 'Red Star', burgundy foliage; and 'Pink Stripe' in shades of shrieking cerise. *Cordyline indivisa* (Z9) has broader green foliage and tends, when young, to be less hardy. *C. australis*, 'Atropurpurea' and *C. indivisa* can be propagated by seed, but the fancy types are best purchased.

The brilliantly coloured *Cordyline* 'Pink Stripe' is well worth growing but likely to be less hardy than the plain green species.

Cortaderia

Graminae/Poaceae

Totally Hardy

The pampas grasses have been much maligned for being unfashionable. Ignore that – they are excellent, exotic looking grasses. All make impressive clumps of wiry evergreen foliage, topped in late summer by stately spires of ivory white flowers. The species *Cortaderia selloana* (Z7) makes a great statement reaching to a towering 2.75m (9ft) when in full flower. 'Sunningdale Silver' AGM is shorter at 1.5m (5ft). For colourful foliage, grow 'Gold Band' (syn 'Aureolineata' AGM) or 'Silver Stripe', both of which are more compact at just over 1m (4ft). Flowers are not as showy as the green-leaved ones. Use pampas either as part of background planting or as features in grass or low planting. They prefer full sun but are not fussy about soil. However do give them plenty of space, as the foliage spreads. Propagate by division in spring.

This bright yellow *Crocosmia* 'Citronella' contrasts well with the tall dark foliage of *Phormium tenax* 'Atropurpurea', growing behind.

Cosmos

Asteraceae/Compositae

Half Hardy

A genus of daisies included mainly for *Cosmos atrosanguineus* (Z10), sometimes called the chocolate plant because of its sweet evocative scent. Originates from Mexico where it is sadly almost extinct. This plant grows from small tubers, producing slender stems with single daisy-like flowers in deepest maroon. About 45cm (18in) tall. Curious and a sharp contrast to paler colours. Treat rather like a dahlia by overwintering the tubers under frost-free conditions. Can be propagated from spring cuttings of new growth. Also *Cosmos bipinnatus* (Z10), a group of fast growing, seed raised annuals with daisy flowers in pinks and whites. The cultivar 'Sonata White' is particularly striking.

Crocosmia

Iridaceae

Totally Hardy

Although originating from South Africa, these colourful plants are totally hardy. They grow from corms, producing narrow sword-shaped green leaves with summer flowers in shades of red, orange and yellow. Each flower spike produces many small flowers, which results in a long season of display. They grow to around 90cm (3ft). 'Lucifer' AGM (Z6) is a readily available and reliable cultivar with bright scarlet flowers, and *C. X crocosmiiflora* 'Solfatare' AGM (Z6) is a good golden yellow with the bonus of lightly bronzed foliage. Propagate by separating out crowded clumps of corms in spring.

Cycas

Cycadaceae

Bordeline Hardy

These are a group of fossil plants that date back to the Jurassic period. Although in the past only regularly seen in greenhouses in botanic gardens, they are now more readily available, and some adventurous gardeners are gambling with them outside. *Cycas revoluta* AGM (Z9), the sago palm is the most readily available. This makes a spreading, shuttlecock-shaped plant like the top of a truncated palm with long, wiry glossy pinnate green leaves. In a cold winter, the foliage may be damaged to the point of complete loss, but its habit of producing a complete new circle of foliage in one growth spurt means that it will recover again in most years. Excellent drainage with extra grit and sand, combined with a light covering of horticultural fleece in freezing weather, is the secret to success with these unusual plants.

Cyperus

Cyperaceae

Half Hardy

This genus is included mainly for the graceful *Cyperus papyrus* AGM (Z10), commonly known as the source of early Egyptian paper. This aquatic plant makes tall leafless stems crowned with shaggy heads of hair-thin green filaments. A good established plant will make a striking specimen up to nearly 2m (6ft) tall. This plant needs constant moisture, so ideally grow as a marginal in the damp soil at the edge of a pool. Alternatively grow in a large pot and plunge this in a container of water, which in turn can be buried to hide it. It is not frost hardy, so plants must be returned to a frost-free greenhouse, around 10°C (50°F) for the winter. Mature plants set seed easily, and this can be used to raise young plants for the future. You may also like to try growing *Cyperus involucratus* AGM (Z10) (syn *alternifolius*), the umbrella plant, which does not grow as tall and is topped with broader leaf-like bracts.

Dahlia

Asteraceae/Compositae

Half Hardy

This vast group of highly colourful plants is featured on page 47. Dahlias were originally introduced to the UK from Mexico in 1798. Although there are only around thirty native species this genus has been highly hybridized, and records now show over 20,000 named cultivars, classified in groups. Gardeners tend to love or loathe them. Very few of the true species are now grown, although *Dahlia coccinea* is worth trying, with attractive small, single red flowers. *D. imperialis*, otherwise known as the tree dahlia, will

DESIRABLE DAHLIAS

Name	Colour	Type	Foliage	Height
'Arabian Knight'	Deep ruby	Decorative	Green	over 1m (4ft)
'Bishop of Llandaff' AGM	Scarlet	Single	Bronze	90cm (3ft)
'David Howard' AGM	Orange	Miniature decorative	Bronze	over 1m (4ft)
'Moonfire' AGM	Orange and red	Single	Bronze	90cm (3ft)
'Roxy'	Cerise	Single	Bronze	90cm (3ft)
'Berger's Rekord'	Scarlet	Cactus flowered	Green	90cm (3ft)
'Golden Emblem'	Yellow	Decorative	Green	90cm (3ft)

Most commercially available *Dasylirions* are hybrids, but they are still excellent garden plants particularly for desert landscapes.

achieve 2.75m (9ft) in the season, making a striking specimen foliage plant but sadly rarely producing its pink flowers in cool areas. All are very tender so regard as Z10.

Dasylirion

Ruscaceae

Generally Hardy to Borderline Hardy

These are wonderfully spiky plants forming a 90cm (3ft) fountain of silvery grey foliage. The naming of them is a nightmare and most of the stocks that appear in many nurseries are likely to be hybrids of unknown parentage. Blue foliage types are likely to include parentage of *D. glaucophyllum* (Z9) and types with toothed foliage, *D. serratifolium* (Z9). If you can get it, the species, *Dasylirion wheeleri* AGM (Z8) is likely to be hardy. Give them full sun and excellent drainage.

Dicksonia

Dicksoniaceae

Borderline Hardy

The tree ferns are generally represented in many gardens by *Dicksonia antarctica* AGM (Z9) from New Zealand. This primitive plant makes an impressive specimen. It can be obtained in many sizes but is usually purchased as a leafless trunk, which must be kept moist. It is proving to be tougher and hardier under temperate conditions than expected, but it is still worth protecting the growing point over winter with a handful of straw. Grow in semi-shade. Most of these are imported from Tasmania, where they are salvaged under licence from land clearance projects. Can be propagated by spores, but for practical purposes this plant is probably best purchased.

Dodonea

Sapindaceae

Half Hardy

The hopbush, *Dodonea viscosa* is a common tree in hot arid areas and a native to southern California and parts of Mexico. 'Purpurea' (Z10), which has rich bronze foliage is the best form to grow in gardens. If grown as a tender perennial and planted out for summer display, it produces a shapely spire of narrow purple foliage and possibly pink flowers. May be worth trying outside over winter in sheltered locations. Propagate by semi-ripe cuttings in the autumn.

Ensete

Musaceae

Half Hardy

A group of tropical bananas originating from Africa, Madagascar and southern Asia. All have huge paddle-like leaves growing from a trunk-like false stem composed of the bases of leaf stalks. The growing point is actually at ground level, making them giant herbaceous perennials.

The most familiar is *Ensete ventricosum* AGM (Z10), the Abyssinian banana. This is a magnificent foliage plant that has been valued since Victorian times, when it was widely grown. It is a fast growing species and very rewarding to grow, reaching 3m (10ft) or more, with leaves as much as nearly 2m (6ft) long and 60cm (2ft) wide. It eventually has cup-shaped flowers followed by banana-like fruits that are dry and quite inedible. Plant in sheltered locations to avoid leaves shredding.

Propagate from seed sown in early spring, and it will make a leafy plant about 90cm (3ft) in height by late summer. Although easy and fast growing, it is quite tender so will not survive outside, even with protection. It needs a heated greenhouse with a temperature of at least 10°C (50°F). During the second season it really gets going, making a spectacular plant. Mature plants become difficult to overwinter because of their immense size, but as the growing point is at ground level they can be cut hard back to stumps no more than 20cm (8in) tall and will usually re-sprout again. Such treatment solves the overwintering problem but means that we lose some of the stature of a mature plant.

E. ventricosum 'Maurelii' (Z10), the red Abyssinian banana is possibly the most spectacular of all the ornamental bananas, with huge leaves richly coloured in shades of red, ruby, chocolate through to almost black. Although not as big as the species, it still makes a massive specimen with a considerable impact in any garden. Tends to be more tender than the species, so requires an overwinter temperature of at least 13°C (55°F) (for propagation, *see* page 67). The same plant is also sometimes renamed by the nursery trade as

Ensete ventricosa 'Montbeliardii' is similar to the more common 'Maurelii but has narrower leaves and the foliage colour is often a richer purple.

'Santa Morelli' or 'Tandara Red', an annoying habit aimed at increasing sales.

E. ventricosum 'Montbeliardii' (Z10) is very similar to 'Maurelii' but is taller, generally more slender and reputed to be more richly coloured. This is a reintroduction of an old cultivar thought to have been lost.

Equisetum

Equisetaceae

Totally Hardy

These are the horsetails, primitive plants of a very

invasive nature, some of which are pernicious weeds, so use with care. Included here for *Equisetum hyemale* (Z3), a curious plant with nearly 90cm (3ft) tall thin green leafless stems, like giant chives, ringed with bands of cream and black. Grow in a pot to avoid it spreading, and stand in a container of water to keep constantly moist. Slender stems are fragile so handle with care. Cut back in spring if it gets untidy, and propagate by division.

Erythrina

Leguminosae/Papilionaceae

Half Hardy

The coral trees are a striking sight in warm climates with their brilliant, often red or pink flowers. Try *Erythrina crista-gali* (Z9), the cockspur coral tree, which is the easiest to grow in temperate conditions. It will survive in a pot and will usually flower with spectacular crimson flowers when quite small. It is deciduous so drops its leaves in the winter, when it should be kept under frost free glass. There is a form called 'Compacta', that seems to be superior for pot culture.

Eschscholtzia

Papaveraceae

Generally Hardy

Included for *Eschscholtzia californica* (Z8), the Californian poppy, a short, fast growing annual, producing delicate silvery foliage and silky flowers in reds, oranges, yellows or cream. It fits in well in an arid garden, which mimics the desert surroundings from which it originates. If you have sown it or planted it once, it will seed freely in future years. However it is not invasive, as unwanted seedlings are easily removed. In an arid garden, which is often primarily green or silver, the touches of brilliant colour are most effective.

Eucalyptus

Myrtaceae

Totally to Generally Hardy

This is a huge group of evergreen trees, mostly with aromatic, silver foliage and generally originating in Australia. They are widely used as landscape plants in many warm areas. There are a number which are hardy enough to include in temperate landscapes. Most are fast-growing, achieving 20–30m (75–100ft) in a few years. They generally respond well to hard pruning, so can be easily kept at a reasonable size. In fact many have different juvenile foliage which is more attractive than that on a mature tree, and hard pruning will stimulate this.

The pineapple lily, *Eucomis bicolor*, is an exotic bulb from South Africa, that is hardy in most areas and flowers in mid-summer.

Eucalyptus gunnii AGM (Z7) is readily available and makes a conical tree with peeling pinkish cream bark. The foliage is silvery blue and round when young, turning more sickle-shaped when older. The snow gum, *E. pauciflora* subsp *niphophila* AGM (Z8), makes a quite spreading tree, again with flaking bark and reddish stems, contrasting with the silver foliage. *Eucalyptus periniana* (Z8) has juvenile leaves that completely encircle the stem, which grows through the centre of each round leaf. As the leaf dies and dries, it becomes partially detached from the stem and blows in the wind, giving it the common name 'spinning gum'. All of these are hardy enough to grow as permanent trees in the exotic garden. You can raise the fast-growing *E. globulus* (Z8), the blue gum, from seed each year and use as a summer display plant, reaching just under 2m (6ft) in a season.

Eucalyptus are propagated by seed and do not respond well to transplanting, so they should be planted as young plants direct from a small container before becoming pot bound.

Eucomis

Hyacinthaceae/Liliaceae

Generally Hardy

The pineapple lilies are summer flowering bulbs which originate from South Africa and are becoming increasingly popular with the current taste for the exotic. The most readily available is *Eucomis bicolor* AGM (Z8), which is stocked by most bulb merchants and garden centres. It makes a plant about 45cm (18in) tall topped with spikes of greenish white flowers marked with purple. Each spike is topped with a little tuft of pineapple-like foliage, which gives the plant its common name. *E. comosa* (Z8) is also fairly easy to obtain and similar, but with purple spotted stems and white flowers that are tinted with pink. The cultivar 'Sparkling Burgundy' produces rich ruby red leaves and huge flower spikes in bright cerise pink. It is sometimes sold purely as 'Purple Form'. You can plant them in a sunny well-drained site outside or alternatively grow them in pots, starting under glass and moving outside for the summer. If planted out, mulch well before winter.

Euphorbia

Euphorbiaceae

Totally to Generally Hardy

Most of those included here are sub-shrubs. *Euphorbia characias* (Z7) is available in several forms such as 'Lambrook Gold' AGM and the spectacular 'John Tomlinson' AGM. All make shapely globes of silvery foliage about 90cm (3ft) in height, topped in spring with rounded heads of long-lasting, limey yellow bracts. There is a fine variegated form, cumbersomely named *E. characias* subsp. *wulfenii* 'Emmer Green'. *E. mellifera* AGM (Z8) grows to just over 1m (4ft) with apple green foliage clearly marked with a strong white central vein. The insignificant flowers are strongly scented with honey.

Euphorbias should be pruned after flowering by removing all the stems that have finished flowering, leaving new shoots for next year. Propagate by means of semi-ripe cuttings in the autumn. However, be aware that all euphorbias have a poisonous and irritant white sap, which should not get on your skin or eyes, so wear gloves when handling and take great care.

Fargesia

Graminae/Poaceae

Totally Hardy

A group of fairly vigorous, clump forming and well-behaved bamboos. *Fargesia murieliae* AGM (Z7) is an elegant and easy bamboo with tall thin, gently swaying canes, growing to 2.5m (8ft) or more. 'Jumbo' is a vigorous clone and very hardy, broader leaved and may achieve 4m (13ft). *Fargesia nitida*

Fascicularia **species are bromeliads that are virtually hardy, and once established in a sunny location provide a colourful summer display.**

AGM (Z7) is very similar to *F. murieliae* but with more upright canes and a purplish hue from the second year, also growing to 4m (13ft). Sadly, they sometimes have the annoying habit of flowering, seeding and dying when mature.

Fascicularia

Bromeliaceae

Generally Hardy

This is a hardy bromeliad from Chile, which is amazingly tough and easy to grow under temperate conditions. There is some confusion between two very similar species, *Fascicularia bicolor* ssp *bicolor* (syn *pitcairnifolia*) (Z8) and *F. bicolor* ssp c*analiculata* (Z8), although the latter appears to be freer flowering. Both have rosettes of spiky green foliage, no more than 45cm (18in) tall. Eventually small blue flowers will appear in the centre, at which time the central leaves turn bright scarlet. Plant in a hot, well-drained, sunny location or keep in a pot. If in doubt before winter, protect with a loose covering of fleece or a tuft of straw in the centre of each crown.

Fatsia

Araliaceae

Totally Hardy

Broad shiny leaved evergreens that are useful for background planting. *Fatsia japonica* AGM (Z7), the Japanese aralia, makes a rounded bush growing to as much as 3m (10ft) with glossy green, deeply lobed leaves. In late summer, clouds of tiny, rather dirty white flowers are produced, followed by round black fruits. There is a variegated form simply known as 'Variegata' AGM and a lovely but slow growing golden leaved cultivar called 'Anelise'. All very tough and tolerant, but variegated types prefer a sunny location for best leaf colour. The species can be propagated by seed and the cultivars by cuttings.

Ficus

Moraceae

Totally Hardy and Half Hardy

This is the genus that contains both the edible fig and the houseplants known as rubber plants. *Ficus carica* (Z7), the edible fig is worth including in an exotic garden for its three or five lobed leaves, much loved by the sculptors of classical statues. It can be grown as a free standing tree but is probably better trained against a wall. It will easily achieve 3m (10ft) or more. There are many different fruiting cultivars, although

The fruiting fig, *Ficus carica*, is a classic plant with large exotic leaves that is best grown trained against a warm wall.

the most common is 'Brown Turkey' AGM. Fig trees are hardy, but the young embryonic fruit is produced the year before ripening and may need protecting over winter.

The once popular rubber plant, *Ficus elastica* (Z10), that graced many houses in the 1960s and 1970s is a large leaved but tender plant that can also be used outside in the summer. Coloured leaved cultivars such as 'Variegata', 'Doescheri' AGM and 'Belize' can be quite spectacular when grown with other exotics. Do be sure to carefully acclimatize them to outdoor conditions and either plant them in a lightly shaded location with moist soil or keep in their pots. They must go back to a heated greenhouse before cold weather in the autumn. You can also try *Ficus benjamina* AGM (Z9), the weeping fig and *Ficus pumila* AGM (Z7), the creeping fig. The latter is a small spreading plant which, if allowed to climb on a sunny, sheltered wall, may survive outdoors over winter. All propagated by cuttings.

Fremontodendron

Sterculiaceae

Generally Hardy

These shrubs are known for their golden yellow, cup shaped flowers produced profusely in early summer. *Fremontodendron californicum* 'California Glory' AGM (Z8) is probably one of the best and readily available. They are best grown against a warm wall, both for

protection and support, as the plant is vigorous and can achieve 4m (13ft). Be warned that all fremontodendrons have foliage and shoots with irritant hairs.

Fuchsia

Onagraceae

Half Hardy

Most fuchsias are too dainty for the exotic garden, but a few of the less usual types can be of use. *Fuchsia boliviana* makes a small dishevelled tree, up to 1m (4ft)

Grevillea 'Canberra Gem' comes from Australia but is totally hardy and produces a continuous show of curious flowers throughout the early summer.

tall, with huge trusses of fluorescent red trumpets. You may also like the unusual *F. splendens (syn cordifolia)* with long red trumpets tipped with green. The triphylla hybrids such as 'Thalia' AGM, 'Koralle and 'Gartenmeister Bonstedt' AGM, in shades of brick red and orange with bronze foliage, are quite handsome for summer colour. Coloured leaved foliage types such as 'Firecracker', 'Genii' AGM and 'Autumnale' AGM are also useful for underplanting. Most of these grow to about 45cm (18in), although 'Autumnale' is more prostrate. These are all Z10, although there are also some hardy types. All are grown from autumn or spring tip cuttings and must be overwintered under frost-free glass for planting out in the summer.

Grevillea

Proteaceae

Borderline Hardy and Half Hardy

There are many species of *Grevillea*, most of which originate from Australia, and sadly only a few are tough enough for temperate areas. 'Canberra Gem' AGM (Z9) makes a light feathery shrub with slender branches covered in narrow needle-like green foliage and clusters of spidery pink flowers. The cultivar 'Olympic Flame' is similar, and *G. juniperina* f. *sulphurea* (Z9) has yellow flowers. All prefer a sunny sheltered spot and are hardy enough to remain outdoors permanently, growing to around 1.5m (5ft).

Grevillea robusta AGM (Z11), the silk oak is much more tender and can only be used as a summer visitor. It makes a narrow upright plant, clothed in finely cut, greenish bronze foliage. A two-year-old plant will make just under 2m (6ft) of growth. It has been used as a dot plant for summer bedding for years – understated but rather refined! In warmer climates it makes a very tall and graceful tree, but permanent specimens in cool areas are very limited and only in especially favourable locations. Worth a try though if you want to leave a plant in place. It is propagated from seed, but it is quite slow so you will need to wait to the second year for a usable plant.

Griselinia

Griselinaceae

Generally Hardy

A genus of wonderfully glossy leaved evergreen shrubs from New Zealand. *Griselinia littoralis* AGM (Z8) makes a rounded shrub with leathery bright green leaves, eventually growing to about 3m (10ft). It is totally hardy but best thought of as a background plant. There is a familiar variegated form, but it is preferable to search for the more refined 'Dixon's Cream' or 'Bantry Bay', both of which have attractive cream leaf markings and are more compact. *Griselinia lucida* (Z9) is slightly more tender but has nicely rounded leaves, the colour of a Granny Smith apple. Propagate by semi-ripe cuttings in autumn.

Gunnera

Gunneraceae

Totally Hardy

Included mainly for the herbaceous perennial, *Gunnera manicata* AGM (Z6), (syn *G. brasiliensis*) sometimes known as giant rhubarb, although it is not related to the edible type. This foliage plant, from Brazil, grows to 2m (7ft) or more and produces huge rugged-looking leaves which can themselves be over 1.5m (5ft) across. It needs plenty of space and grows best in a permanently damp soil, such as the edge of a pool or stream. Although hardy, it is worth protecting the crowns over winter, using the old cut-down foliage in the autumn. Propagate by seed or division.

Hedychium

Zingiberaceae

Generally Hardy

These are the ornamental gingers, grown for their

The contrasting colours of *Helichrysum petiolare* 'Limelight' and *Strobilanthes dyerana* make perfect exotic groundcovers under tall species.

exotic green foliage and highly fragrant late summer flowers. All grow from fleshy rhizomes (mostly Z8), and their culture is very similar to cannas. There are many different types, such as the pale yellow *H. gardnerianum* AGM, the white *H. coronarium* and the orange flowered *H. coccineum* 'Tara' AGM. 'Assam Orange', which is a cultivar of *H. densiflorum,* has tightly packed spikes of deep orange flowers, and *H. greenii* has almost red flowers and the bonus of glossy green foliage, with a deep maroon underside – another plant to be appreciated lying on your back! Most grow to about 1.5m (5ft). Look out for some of the spectacular new hybrids produced by Tom Wood, an American hybridist. Grow in an open sunny location and either mulch the roots well over winter or dig and store like cannas. Propagate by dividing the rhizomes in spring.

Helichrysum

Asteraceae/Compositae

Half Hardy

Just one species of interest to us here, namely *Helichrysum petiolare* AGM (Z10). This is a fast-growing tender silver foliage plant that makes an excellent cushion of small silver leaves. No more than 30cm (1ft) tall but can easily spread to 90cm (3ft). The cultivar 'Limelight' AGM has greenish golden foliage. Both make excellent foils for brightly coloured plants. They are totally tender, so must be overwintered under glass. Propagate from softwood cuttings in spring.

Hibanobambusa

Graminae/Poaceae

Generally Hardy

Included for a naturally occurring hybrid called *Hibanobambusa tranquillans* 'Shiroshima' AGM (Z8). This is one of the best variegated bamboos with large, glossy green leaves with creamy variegations, growing to 2m (7ft) or more. The canes are attractively grooved on one side. It has an active habit but is easily controlled and is tolerant of dry conditions.

Humulus

Cannabaceae

Totally Hardy

Beer drinkers will no doubt know the value of hops, but the one of interest to us here is the golden foliage form, *Humulus lupulus* 'Aureus' AGM (Z4). This is a hardy herbaceous climber, which can reach 6m (20ft) in a single season, covered in rich golden foliage. It dies back to the ground each winter and can be propagated by division.

Ipomoea

Convolvulaceae

Half Hardy

A curious genus with many climbers, of which the most familiar is probably the morning glory, *Ipomoea tricolor* (Z10), a short-lived climbing annual with vivid, mainly blue trumpet flowers. *Ipomoea lobata* (Z10), (syn *Mina lobata*) is another useful climber with small but brilliant orange and cream flowers. Under ideal conditions they can make 3m (10ft) in a season. Both are easily grown from seed sown under heated glass in the spring.

Various ornamental foliage forms of *Ipomoea batatas* (Z10), the sweet potato, have appeared in recent years and are also very useful. These include several almost black cultivars such as the delicate leaved 'Blackie' and very similar 'Sweet Caroline Purple' and then the broad leaved forms such as 'Black Tone' and 'Sweetheart Purple'. Lime green forms are available including 'Marguerite' and 'Sweetheart Light Green', both of which have heart-shaped foliage, and the cut-leaved form 'Sweet Caroline Light Green'. This complexity of names may simply be the vagaries of different suppliers. There is also a rather delicate pink and white variegated form quite simply called 'Tricolor' and a new bronze-leaved cultivar named 'Sweet Caroline Bronze'. All make spreading plants, no more than 30cm (1ft) tall, covered with sumptuous foliage, good either as groundcover or as container plants. All are grown from spring cuttings or plugs.

Iresine

Amaranthaceae

Half Hardy

A genus of tender but brilliantly coloured foliage plants. *Iresine herbstii* 'Brilliantissimum' is the brightest, with almost neon cerise and deep ruby leaves, sometimes called the beefsteak plant. Once again plant distributors have annoyingly renamed it, and you may find it offered under the name 'Blazin' Rose'. Its counterpart, *Iresine* 'Aureo Reticulata', now also sold as 'Blazin' Lime', has lime green leaves, vividly veined with lemon yellow and hints of cerise. There is also a taller cultivar with narrow deep purple leaves called 'Lindenii' AGM. All make vibrant contributions

Iresine herbstii **'Brilliantissimum' exhibits its vivid colours against the muted green of the large leaved** *Pelargonium papilionaceum.*

to the summer display and will reach about 45cm (18in) in a season. All Z11. Easy to propagate by spring cuttings but must be overwintered under heated glass at 10°C (50°F) or higher.

Kniphofia

Asphodelaceae/Liliaceae

Totally Hardy

This familiar group of 'old fashioned' garden plants are commonly known as red hot pokers. Not necessarily a good description, as these plants are now available in tantalizing shades of orange, yellow and cool limey green. Hardly 'red hot' but the spiky foliage

and bright flowers are distinctly exotic. The species mostly come from rough grasslands in Africa but many have been hybridized in recent years. Some are evergreen and some deciduous, all with narrow linear foliage. All produce tall spikes of small tubular flowers.

The cultivar 'Royal Standard' AGM (Z6) is a typical traditional 'poker' with a two-tone flower head, deep red buds at the top of the spike opening to orange and yellow flowers. It grows to around 90cm (3ft). If you want an all red one, try 'Prince Igor' (Z6), which is tall at nearly 2m (6ft). For a clear soft orange, plant 'Bees' Sunset' AGM (Z6). Use kniphofias towards the back of the border, as their foliage is not always tidy, and plant a soft cushioning plant such as the silver *Centaurea gymnocarpa* in front to hide the base. Although they prefer a moist, humus-rich soil, once established they are very tolerant of hot dry conditions. Propagate by division in spring.

Koelreuteria

Sapindaceae

Totally Hardy

Included for the species *Koelreuteria paniculata* AGM (Z5), the golden rain tree, which should be more widely grown. The foliage is handsome with finely toothed pinnate leaves. In midsummer, the tree produces lacy panicles of golden yellow flowers, which *en masse* are quite spectacular. In the autumn it has a bonus of golden autumn tints before the foliage drops. It can eventually reach 10m (30ft) but is relatively slow growing and so suitable for a small garden. It flowers when quite young.

Lantana

Verbenaceae

Half Hardy

These small shrubby perennials form a major part of

many exotic landscapes in warmer countries, where their vivid colours and constant flowering is much valued. Under temperate conditions, they have to be overwintered under heated glass and planted out for summer display. Their two-tone flowers are particularly fascinating, instructing insects as to which flowers are still waiting for pollination. The foliage is pleasantly aromatic. The taller bushy types are cultivars of *Lantana camara* (Z11) and there are many named forms. Plants will probably make 45cm (18in) in a season, but older overwintered plants can get much bigger. There is also a carpeting species, *L. montevidensis* (Z11) which is pale lavender, and a white version of it. Lantanas are easily propagated by softwood cuttings taken in autumn and overwintered under heated glass at around 10°C (50°F). Unfortunately they are particularly prone to damage by whitefly and red spider mite. All parts of the plant are highly poisonous.

Ligustrum

Oleaceae

Generally to Totally Hardy

Another group of plants known for its poor cousin, in this case the common privet, mindlessly used for dreary hedging. This humble subject has a number of superior relatives that are well worth while growing in the exotic garden.

One favourite is *L. lucidum* AGM (Z8), the Chinese privet. This makes a large shrub or ultimately a small tree up to 10m (30ft). It has handsome glossy evergreen foliage and in late summer produces tapering panicles of delicate, tiny creamy-white flowers, which are followed by black berries. There is a yellow variegated form called 'Excelsum Superbum' AGM, and there is another called 'Tricolor', which has white variegated leaves with touches of pink and is a bit inclined to be tender. *L. japonicum* (Z7) is a similar evergreen but only growing to about 3m (10ft). All these choice 'privets' make good background or specimen shrubs, even small trees, and once estab-

lished are very tolerant of dry conditions including partial shade. Propagate by semi-ripe cuttings in autumn.

Lilium

Liliaceae

Totally Hardy

A huge genus of bulbous plants, with numerous species and cultivars, many of which are colourful enough to include in the exotic garden. They are probably most useful as mid-season filler plants, and on that basis are probably best pot grown. Plant individual bulbs into 12cm (5in) pots using a well-drained compost. Most lilies are totally hardy so they can be started off outside in a sheltered location. When the young growth has emerged, you can move them to their summer flowering location or leave them in their pots until the flowering stage and use them as fillers, wherever you have a gap needing some exotic colour.

Lobelia

Campanulaceae

Totally to Generally Hardy

The plants of interest to us here are the herbaceous lobelias, which are tall upright growing plants. *Lobelia cardinalis* 'Queen Victoria' AGM (Z4) grows to about 45cm (18in) with deep bronze foliage topped with rich scarlet flowers. The more recent cultivar 'Elmfeuer' is very similar but an overall improvement. Both are propagated by division or bought as plugs. There are also several seed raised strains such as the 'Fan Series' and 'Compliment Series' (Z4), both of which have green foliage and spires of colourful flowers in red, pink or blue. Although hardy, all are best treated as bedding plants and raised from seed, plugs or divisions. *Lobelia tupa* (Z8) is also worth considering.

Growing to about 1m (3ft) in height, *Melianthus major* makes a striking mound of crisply cut silvery blue foliage.

It is a stately, clump forming perennial, growing to as much as 1.5m (5ft) with spikes of curious dark red flowers.

Melianthus

Melianthaceae

Generally Hardy

The star here is *Melianthus major* AGM (Z8), a relaxed sub-shrub with handsome, finely toothed grey foliage. Although it does flower with small, dark brownish red flowers, these are not produced until very late in the season and are rather insignificant. Grows to 1.5m (5ft) or more and looks particularly good as a contrast against bright colours and dark foliage. Although a beautiful plant, the foliage has a pungent smell, so plant away from the front of the border. Grow in a sunny sheltered location and mulch well in the autumn, to protect the root system and basal shoots. In mild winters, the top growth will survive and it will make quite a sizeable plant. In a tough winter, the top growth will die down but it will usually re-sprout from the base. In some situations it will send out runners freely. Propagate from seed or by softwood cuttings of young shoots in the spring.

Miscanthus

Graminae/Poaceae

Totally Hardy

The Japanese silver grasses are a large group of clump-forming grasses mostly growing to around 1.5m (5ft) tall. Many have fine foliage and produce loosely arching plumes like distorted paintbrushes. Often the variegated miscanthus do not flower as freely as the green leaved ones, but their boldly striped leaves more than compensate for this. Most species are frost hardy (Z5) and clump forming, so generally well-behaved.

There are many species and cultivars. *Miscanthus sacchariflorus* is a tall, green-leaved species but it is not fully hardy. The broad, arching leaves make it useful as a screen or background plant, growing to 3m (10ft). *Miscanthus sinensis* 'Variegatus' is probably the most widely grown of the coloured leaved miscanthus, although the cultivar 'Feecy' is an improvement. Both grow to about 90cm (3ft). For a taller variegated grass try *Miscanthus sinensis* 'Cabaret', which has thick ribbon-like foliage with bold milky white, linear centres and dark green leaf margins. 'Cosmopolitan' AGM is very similar, and both grow to nearly 2m (6ft). *Miscanthus sinensis* 'Zebrinus' AGM, zebra grass has green leaves conspicuously banded with gold, growing to over 1m (4ft). All prefer a moist, well-drained soil and a sunny situation. Propagate by division in late spring.

Musa

Musaceae

Generally Hardy to Half Hardy

The true bananas are a genus of tender herbaceous perennials. In the garden, they are grown for their gigantic paddle-shaped leaves, produced from a false stem, giving a tree-like effect. Small tubular flowers are eventually formed with coloured bracts. After flowering, the shoot will die, usually to be replaced by suckers from the base.

Undoubtedly the most useful for the exotic garden is *M. basjoo* AGM (Z8), the so-called hardy banana. This is a suckering perennial with slender false stems which are green when young and eventually turn papery brown. Leaves are bright green and huge, on a giant plant growing to 5m (16ft) or more. Cream flowers are followed by yellowish green fruit – which is full of black seeds and unpalatable. This is one of the hardiest of all bananas and can be planted permanently in the garden (*see* page 84 for overwintering). *M. sikkimensis* (Z9) makes a similar dramatic plant with glossy leaves up to nearly 2m (6ft) long and with a distinct purple flush on the underside.

Although you cannot expect edible bananas, flowering shoots on *Musa basjoo* are fascinating features.

The zebra banana, *Musa zebrina* is tender and so can only be planted out for the summer months, but it's still worth the extra effort.

The species can be variable, and some seedlings may even have strong chocolate-coloured markings on the young leaves. It is also tough enough to grow outside and tends to be more wind resistant than *M. basjoo*. Protect the stem and roots over winter as described for *M. basjoo*.

Amongst the tender species, *Musa velutina* AGM (Z10), the hot pink banana is a fun plant to grow. It is easily grown from seed, and it flowers and fruits as a quite young plant, often within the first year at around 1.5m (5ft) tall. It has glossy green foliage with a reddish tinge to the petioles and pseudostem. The flowers, when they appear are bright pink in colour and followed by small velvety pink, inedible bananas full of small black seeds. You may also like to try *M. acuminata* 'Zebrina' AGM (Z11), the blood banana. This striking plant has broad leaves, irregularly splashed with dark red or purple. It is being offered through the trade under the inaccurate name of 'Santa Zebrina'. It can grow up to 3m (10ft) or more. Being totally tender, it must be overwintered under heated glass, at about 10°C (50°F) and just planted out for the summer.

If you want edible bananas, *M. acuminata* 'Dwarf Cavendish' AGM (Z11) produces them. It can be planted out for the summer and makes a handsome plant with bright green leaves flushed with purple-red markings. Grows to about 1.5m (5ft) and eventually forms pendant clusters of yellow flowers with purple bracts. The fruit is seedless and about 20cm (8in) long with sweet flesh. It needs a minimum winter temperature of 10°C (50°F). The cultivar known as 'Super Dwarf Cavendish' is often available in garden centres, as a small, novel pot plant, less than 25cm (9in) tall. In warmer climates it makes an unusual groundcover plant.

Most species can be planted out for summer display in exotic schemes. They prefer full sun or light shade and a moist soil. A sheltered position is preferable, as strong winds will shred the leaves. Although some bananas can be successfully grown outdoors in temperate climates utilizing simple protection, tender species must be lifted, potted and overwintered under frost-free glass. Most bananas produce suckers which can be separated in the spring and grown on to form new plants. They can also be propagated from seed, which should be soaked in warm water for 24 hours before germinating at 21°C (70°F). Bananas can be attacked by red spider mite, mealy bug and aphid, particularly when grown under glass.

The huge yellow flowers on *Musella lasiocarpa*, sometimes called the water lily banana, are showy and will last for several months.

Musella

Musaceae

Half Hardy

The Chinese yellow banana *M. lasiocarpa* (Z10) originates from China and has over the years been classified as both *Musa* and *Ensete* before getting a genus of its own. It grows to nearly 2m (6ft) with a stiff shape, a chunky false stem and stiff leaves held like a shuttlecock. It flowers when relatively young, with a spectacular yellow inflorescence like a giant, golden water lily that can last for over six months. It works well as a container plant or can be planted out, but must be returned to a frost-free greenhouse for the winter.

Nerium

Apocynaceae

Borderline Hardy

The oleanders are all cultivars of *Nerium oleander* (Z9). Although traditionally regarded as tropical plants, they have proved to be tougher than expected in temperate areas. All make willowy evergreen shrubs with large flower clusters in shades of pink, salmon, white and red. *N. oleander* 'Variegatum' AGM has variegated foliage and pink flowers. Plant in a sheltered spot, ideally against a wall, but if its winter hardiness is in doubt, provide some protection with a wrap of fleece around the branches, packed loosely with straw. They are highly toxic and should be handled with great care.

Amazingly this prickly pear, *Opuntia polycantha*, is not only hardy but will flower outdoors, with yellow trumpets and fruit.

Olea

Oleacea

Generally Hardy

Who would have thought that a book for temperate gardeners could include olive? As a native of Mediterranean areas through to Africa and Australia, it is usually grown in far warmer climates. However as the seasons have altered in temperate areas, it has become quite possible to grow this classic tree.

The olive is *Olea europaea* AGM (Z8), an evergreen tree with leathery greyish leaves. It has tiny white perfumed flowers and is commercially grown for the edible green fruits, which turn black when ripe. Old trees have gnarled shapes and trunks that are full of character. In recent years a trade has developed in old cropped-out olive trees that have been headed back, potted and imported. They can be expensive but provide a great feature tree for an exotic garden. Small low-cost plants are also available and are fast growing.

Opuntia

Cactaceae

Borderline Hardy

This is a typical 'wild west' cactus and very much of a long-shot gamble, as it's a native of Mexico and many need to be kept well above freezing. The hardiest is likely to be *O. robusta* (Z9), the prickly pear, with the typical spiny flat green pads. If you are lucky, yellow flowers and dark red fruits may be produced. *Opuntia polycantha* is a low-spreading species from North America. It has showy yellow flowers and ruby coloured fruits. It is very cold hardy and is said to grow in zones as low as Z3. All opuntias need a very well-drained soil with plenty of grit and a sheltered spot where they will remain dry and warm in winter. Can be protected over winter with an overhead pane of glass to ward off excess rain (*see* cactus feature on page 110 for other species).

Osteospermum

Asteraceae/Compositae

Borderline to Half Hardy

This is a fabulous genus of exotic daisy flowers in a dazzling range of colours. They come mainly from rocky and scrubby areas in South Africa and are hardy only in favourable areas. Some are much tougher than others. *O. jucundum* var. *compactum* AGM (Z9) is one of the toughest and easiest. It is a prostrate, compact plant, covered in bright sugar pink daisies from early summer through to autumn and is very frost hardy. Another one that is virtually hardy is *O. ecklonis* (Z9), which produces white flowers with a blue reverse to the petals, though it is somewhat more straggly in growth. Garden centres often offer numerous other named cultivars that are likely to be less hardy and these should be considered as seasonal plants. Most grow to no more than 30cm (1ft), although some may spread more. All like hot dry locations and will flower best when the soil is poor. Propagate by cuttings in the autumn and overwinter under frost-free glass at around 8°C (45°F).

Paulownia

Scrophulariaceae

Totally Hardy

This genus is known mainly for the foxglove tree, *P. tomentosa* AGM (Z5), which is a native of eastern Asia. It needs long hot dry summers to ripen the wood enough to flower the following year. It flowers in early summer, with masses of showy lilac flowers which can be damaged by late frosts. Allowed to grow freely, it will make a rounded tree, 10m (30ft) or more. In the exotic garden it may be regarded purely as a foliage plant and grown for its huge round dinner-plate leaves, by hard spring pruning, known as stooling (*see* page 24 for more detail).

Pelargonium

Geraniaceae

Half Hardy

These come generally from South Africa and are mainly tender (Z10) but very valuable for the exotic garden and surprisingly will sometimes overwinter in a sheltered spot and a mild winter. There are vast numbers of named cultivars and also species, although the latter are less commonly available.

As well as the flowering types there are also many coloured foliage types such as 'Contrast', 'A Happy Thought' AGM, 'Distinction', 'Madame Salleron' AGM, 'Caroline Schmidt' and 'Vancouver Centennial' AGM. You may also want to use the scented leaved types such as the peppermint scented *P. tomentosum* AGM or the lemon scented *P. crispum* 'Variegatum' AGM, with spires of small round yellow rimmed leaves. Most grow to no more than 45cm (18in). The ivy-leaved types, which are trailing are particularly useful for containers and groundcover. Also try *Pelargonium papilionaceum,* which produces broad vine-like apple green leaves, on a chunky plant. Flowers are small pale pink and insignificant, probably best removed. They are all very tolerant of drought and neglect and particularly useful for containers. All pelargoniums propagate easily by autumn or spring tip cuttings and must be overwintered under glass at around 10°C (50°F).

Pennisetum

Poaceae

Half Hardy

Included here for a couple of particularly attractive foliage grasses. *Pennisetum setaceum* 'Rubrum AGM

OPPOSITE PAGE: ***Pennisetum setaceum*** **'Rubrum', the purple fountain grass is tender but well worth including in summer displays for its foliage and flowers.**

(Z10), the purple fountain grass grows to about 60cm (2ft). The foliage is a rich ruby colour and the flowers are a soft pink. It is not hardy, but well worth including in an exotic scheme. It can be propagated by division and overwintered in a warm greenhouse but tends to be temperamental, so is better bought afresh each year.

'Tall, dark and handsome' neatly describes Millet 'Purple Majesty'. It is actually a cultivar of *Pennisetum glaucum* (Z10), growing to about 90cm (3ft). Mature leaves are long and slender, with a red midrib. It is tall and stately with strong dark flower spikes. The similar 'Purple Baron' is shorter and stockier. Both can be grown from seed each spring, putting two or three seeds in a pot to get a bushy plant. Young plants are green-leaved, but as they mature, exposure to direct sunlight stimulates development of purple leaf colour.

Phoenix

Arecaceae/Palmae

Generally Hardy to Borderline Hardy

The date palms are striking trees when grown in warm climates, and of course they're important fruit crops in some areas. *Phoenix canariensis* AGM (Z8), the Canary Island date palm is the most successful in temperate areas. Reports suggest it will tolerate cold down to as low as –7°C (20°F). It produces long fronds, fringed with rigid green spiny leaves. As a young plant with no trunk, it makes a spreading plant, but mature trees will have fuller heads with some trailing fronds. Eventual height under temperate conditions is unknown. Plant in a good well-drained sunny location, but don't expect to harvest your own dates for a while.

If you want a good palm for a container specimen, try *P. roebelenii* AGM (Z10), the pygmy date palm. This makes a miniature tree, complete with trunk and perfectly shaped head up to around 4m (12ft), although specimens available in nurseries are generally smaller. It is decidedly tender, so do not risk it outside in the winter but bring under frost-free glass for protection.

Phormium tenax 'Maori Sunrise' is one of many cultivars all with a spiky shape and brightly coloured foliage.

Phormium

Agavaceae/Phormiaceae

Generally Hardy

The New Zealand flaxes are a collection of strongly architectural plants with striking, coloured, sword-like foliage. They are technically evergreen herbaceous perennials, so have year-round value.

The hardiest is *Phormium tenax* AGM (Z7). Although this is the plain green species, it makes an immense statuesque plant, with long waving leaves, stretching over 2m (6ft). The flower stems reach up to 3m (10ft) or more with small brick red flowers, which make a pleasant skeletal tracery against the sky. There is a purple-leaved form called 'Purpureum' AGM (Z7) and a variegated form 'Variegatum' AGM (Z7), both of which make slightly smaller plants but still with good characteristics and a robust constitution.

There is now a mouth-watering array of different coloured hybrids, which tend to be less hardy, mostly Z8. 'Yellow Wave' AGM has an arching habit of growth and a rich golden yellow variegation, growing to about 90cm (3ft). There are several with pink tints, including 'Sundowner' AGM, which has an upright habit of growth with leaves that are a soft mix of bronze, olive, red and pink. The cultivar 'Dazzler' has vivid red, pink and green stripes. 'Platt's Black' has to be mentioned as it is the darkest of all and quite compact. And there are many more!

They prefer full sunshine, a sheltered location and good drainage. Once established they are tolerant of dry conditions. The smaller hybrids make fabulous container specimens which can then be planted out when they get too big for their pots. Propagation by division.

Phyllostachys

Graminae/Poaceae

Totally Hardy

A useful group of bamboos with some very attractive stem colours. Probably the best-known member of this genus is *Phyllostachys nigra* AGM, the black bamboo, which is very popular and readily available, with green canes that ripen through purple to deep shiny ebony black by the second or third season. Slender arching habit, to 4m (13ft) and reasonably well-behaved.

Phyllostachys vivax 'Aureocaulis' AGM is possibly the most desirable cultivar, with banana yellow canes, striped with green. It is vigorous and very hardy, with heavy drooping foliage, growing to 4m (13ft). It is inclined to run, but well worth having and controlling. Although not quite so startling, the golden bamboo, *P. aurea* AGM, produces attractive green foliage and grooved, knobbly, green canes fading to gold. It makes a tall screening plant, around 2.5m (8ft) with its best colourings in bright sunlight. 'Albovariegata'

is one of the few tall variegated bamboos, reaching 4m (13ft). All are hardy (Z7). Grow them in an open sunny aspect or light shade, and propagate by division.

Pleioblastus

Graminae/Poaceae

Totally Hardy

Included for *Pleioblastus auricomus* AGM (syn *Arundinaria viridistriata*) (Z7), a delightful compact evergreen bamboo with rich, velvety golden foliage. Needs bright sun and prefers a moist site. Spreading but not over-invasive, it makes an excellent groundcover plant, maximum of 1.5m (5ft). It can be pruned to the ground each spring, for vigorous colourful re-growth.

Plectranthus

Labiatae/Lamiaceae

Half Hardy

A group of tender perennials (Z11), grown for their attractive foliage but confusingly sold in the trade under an array of names. The most familiar is *Plectranthus madagascariensis* 'Variegated Mintleaf' AGM, with green and white foliage and a strongly trailing habit. There is a good compact form with golden leaves sold as 'Sasha' or 'Easy Gold'. Both are useful as an exotic groundcover or in containers. 'Silver Shield' is upright and vigorous with soft silvery leaves and is probably a renaming of *P. argentatus* AGM. It will grow to as much as 45cm (18in) and associates well with bright colours and dark foliage. There is a good variegated form of this called 'Hill House'. All are easy to propagate from tip cuttings but must be overwintered in a greenhouse at around 10°C (50°F). Flowers on all *Plectranthus* are insignificant and should be pinched out.

Pittosporum

Pittosporaceae

Borderline Hardy

This is a genus of elegant, evergreen shrubs mainly from New Zealand. The main display is the foliage but they also have tiny, sweetly scented flowers, followed by sticky black seeds. The most familiar is *Pittosporum tenuifolium* AGM (Z9), which makes a large upright bush or small tree, with delicate green leaves. It may reach 6m (20ft). 'French Lace' is green leaved, but the foliage is slightly smaller than the species, tinged purple and gently wavy. Many coloured-leaf forms are available, including 'Irene Paterson' AGM with silver variegation, and 'Abbotsbury Gold' with yellow blotched leaves. Most of the coloured leaved forms grow to about 2m (7ft) or so. 'Tom Thumb' AGM is not only short and compact, no more than 1m (4ft) but one of very few evergreen plants that has purple foliage.

Somewhat less well known is *P. tobira* AGM (Z9), which makes a small rounded evergreen shrub just over 1m (4ft) tall, with cream scented flowers. There is a good variegated form. Both can be grown in sheltered areas in temperate regions.

They all prefer a moist well-drained soil and sheltered conditions. In particular some of the variegated types can be frost tender in cold areas. Theoretically propagated by autumn cuttings but notoriously difficult to root.

Pseuderanthemum

Acanthaceae

Half Hardy

Included for *Pseuderanthemum* var *atropurpureum* 'Rubrum' (Z11). This plant was, until recently, rarely seen outside conservatory collections but is now often available in garden centres. Glorious, glossy, dark chocolate-coloured foliage with distinct veins. Although relatively slow growing, it will make a bushy plant about 45cm (18in) tall in a season. Good for the front of the border or as a container plant. Propagate by autumn cuttings and overwinter in a warm greenhouse at 13°C (55°F) or warmer.

Pseudopananax

Araliaceae

Generally Hardy to Half Hardy

A group of handsome evergreens from New Zealand, sometimes classified as *Neopanax*, a few of which are almost hardy. Try *Pseudopanax arboreus* (syn *Neopanax arboreus*) (Z9), which has striking, glossy green leaves with five to seven leaflets, growing to nearly 2m (6ft). *Pseudopanax ferox* (Z8) is also hardy and a plant to grow for its curiosity value, rather than its beauty. Its common name of toothed lancewood describes the juvenile foliage, which is serrated like a double-sided freezer knife. The armoury of bronze leaves hang down from its single stem, like a bizarre Christmas tree. Growth is slow, and it takes many years for the plant to mature and start producing the broader adult leaves. Will make say 3m (10ft) growth in ten years. Plant them in a sheltered spot with good drainage and you will find them hardy in most winters.

P. lessonii (Z10) is tender. In particular look out for the spectacular 'Gold Splash' AGM, which makes an upright plant covered with five lobed leaves, generously blotched with gold. It grows well outside in the summer, but must be overwintered under heated glass at around 13°C (55°F).

OPPOSITE PAGE: *Pseudopanax lessonii* 'Goldsplash' is a tall but tender exotic foliage plant, useful for planting amongst shorter species for summer display.

Restios

The restios are a group of evergreen rush-like plants, native mainly to South Africa and Australia. They are part of the fynbos plant community, characterized by a need for natural burning by bush fires. They have only recently been more widely grown and their culture is still a bit experimental, but they are fast becoming the plants that discerning gardeners want.

They vary considerably in appearance, some looking like grasses, others like bamboos or even horsetails. Typically they have striking foliage creating a very dramatic and architectural effect. Most are quite upright in their habit of growth and have very small, much reduced leaves giving them a sparse or feathery appearance. Being relatively new to temperate regions, the hardiness of restios is not yet fully proven, but many gardeners are having considerable success with some species. Most can be regarded as borderline hardiness.

The most familiar is the South African broom reed, *Elegia capensis* (Z9), which has attractive coppery sheaths on bright green stems and grows to nearly 2m (6ft). At a glance it resembles a giant horsetail. The Cape reed, *Rhodocoma gigantea* (Z9) has a much more lush effect like a soft bamboo and will reach 2.5m (9ft) and is likely to be just as hardy. The thatching reed, *Chondropetalum tectorum* (Z9) is by comparison a dumpy little plant at no more than 1m (4ft) tall with spiky grass-like foliage. The plume rush, *Restio tetraphyllus* (Z9), resembles a miniature bamboo. It forms a dense clump of smooth slender stems, with thin, bright green thread-like foliage, carried from about halfway up each stem.

Restios are easy to grow, liking a well-drained but moisture retentive soil. Use a mixture of compost and grit at planting time. Ideally they prefer an acid soil and an open sunny position. Mulch well in the winter and feed sparingly in summer.

Rheum

Polygonaceae

Totally Hardy

These are the rhubarbs, which includes the edible types, although here we are interested in *Rheum palmatum* (Z4), which is a vigorous herbaceous

Restios are a group of South African plants, including this *Elegia capensis*, which are proving remarkably hardy in temperate areas.

perennial. It makes a mound of ruggedly handsome foliage, about 60cm (2ft) tall. The cultivar 'Atro-sanguineum' AGM has brilliant ruby red young foliage fading to green when mature, and red flower buds opening to pink flowers. Well worth growing in a shady damp location. Propagate by division.

Rhodochiton

Plantaginaceae (sometimes classified as Scrophulariaceae)

Half Hardy

Just one species in this genus, Rhodochiton atrosanguineus AGM (syn volubilis) (Z10). Although technically a perennial, this climber is usually grown from seed each year and treated as an annual. In good conditions it can climb to 3m (10ft), producing fascinating two-tone flowers not dissimilar to fuchsias, comprised of a pink calyx, surrounding a deep purple tubular flower. A useful scrambler to grow up through hardy exotics.

Ricinus

Euphorbiaceae

Half Hardy

Although the castor oil plants are sizable shrubs in warm climates, for the exotic garden they are gen-erally grown as annuals from seed. All are cultivars of Ricinus communis (Z10) and rapidly produce eye-catching architectural plants with handsome foliage. 'Carmencita Bright Red' is one of the best, with deep bronze foliage and a bonus of conspicuous prickly red fruits, which follow small flowers in late summer. It can make nearly 2m (6ft) in a good season. 'Impala' is similar but more compact. Look out for the recent introduction, 'New Zealand Purple' with vivid purple foliage. Sow the large seeds in late spring in a warm greenhouse.

Schefflera

Araliaceae

Borderline Hardy and Half Hardy

In the past Scheffleras were considered purely as houseplants. However, species such as S. arboricola AGM (Z10), the umbrella plant, will also grow quite successfully outdoors in the summer. There are some colourful variegated forms of this.

More recently some exciting new introductions have appeared, which are not only quite dramatic but seemingly hardy. The most amazing of these is Schefflera macrophylla (Z9), collected from northern Vietnam. This makes a large shrub, as yet final size unknown, but at least 3m (10ft). Leaves are huge and handsome, comprised of five leaflets on a long and delicate leaf stalk. When the young leaves emerge, they are velvety with an attractive coppery colour which matures to deep green. At the moment, this highly desirable plant is available from very few nurseries and extremely expensive, but it appears to be the new star attraction for the exotic garden.

The similar but less expensive S. delavayi (Z9) and S. taiwaniana (Z9) are also well worth growing for their dramatic shapes and striking foliage. Both have velvety young foliage, although not the same striking colour, and may well prove to be hardy.

Setaria

Graminae/Poaceae

Half Hardy

Included here for the palm grass, Setaria palmifolia (Z10). This grass produces a vigorous clump with broad but linear leaves, conspicuously corrugated along the length. Makes about 45cm (18in) growth. The overall habit is quite elegant, making it a useful groundcover plant under taller species. It is tender, however, so must be returned to a heated green-house, around 8°C (45°F) for the winter. Propagate by division.

Schefflera macrophylla **is a highly desirable recent introduction, making a dramatic hardy plant with impressive foliage.**

Solenostemon

Labiatae/Lamiaceae

Half Hardy

Better known as coleus, these brilliantly coloured, tender foliage plants are excellent additions to the exotic garden. All Z11. Originally popular in the nineteenth century, and often grown as windowsill or conservatory plants, they are equally effective when planted out for summer display. Most grow to around 45cm (18in) and prefer a warm sunny well-drained site. The named cultivars, which have been grown from cuttings, are much better than seed strains, which are inclined to flower and go to seed.

Some of the old Victorian cultivars such as 'Pineapple Beauty' AGM, 'Walter Turner' AGM, 'Crimson Ruffles' AGM and 'Kentish 'Fire' are still available and well worth growing. Modern cultivars include 'Juliet Quartermain', 'Pineapplette' AGM, 'Henna' and 'Saturn'. 'Wisley Tapestry' AGM and 'Red 'Mars' are compact, and 'Lord Falmouth' AGM trails. Naming may vary considerably in the nursery trade. Coleus are all easy to root from tip cuttings but must be kept over winter in a well-heated greenhouse, ideally 16°C (60°F). Because of the expense of this high temperature, they are probably more economically purchased in the spring as plugs.

Sparrmannia

Tiliaceae

Half Hardy

This genus is included for the bold, leafy, but tender shrub *Sparrmannia africana* AGM (Z11). It makes a hefty, upright specimen like a small tree with broad, hairy green leaves. In a good season, it will also produce attractive white flowers with golden stamens, but is worth growing for the foliage alone. Will make nearly 2m (6ft) in a season. Propagate by tip cuttings in the autumn. Reduce the size of the huge leaves by cutting in half across the veins with a sharp knife, before inserting the cuttings. Overwinter in a frost-free greenhouse, around 10°C (50°F) and grow initially as a single stemmed plant to achieve the maximum height.

Stipa

Poaceae

Totally Hardy

A group of fabulous and fashionable grasses, included particularly for the spectacular *Stipa gigantea* AGM (Z5), golden oat grass. It makes large evergreen clumps of narrow grey-green leaves, topped with huge heads of glittering bronze and gilt oat-like flowers in midsummer. Growing to as much as 2m (6ft), it makes a good specimen amongst lower planting and particularly in contrast to broad-leaved species. Plant in an open sunny location and propagate by division or seed in spring.

Strobilanthes

Acanthaceae

Half Hardy

The Persian shield plant, *Strobilanthes dyeriana* AGM (Z10), is another tender foliage plant, grown for its vivid glossy purple and silver leaves with dominant veins. This small, shrubby plant prefers a shady, moist location to produce its best colourings and may then grow to about 90cm (3ft) or more. Propagate by tip cuttings in the autumn, overwinter under warm glass, around 13°C (55°F) and pinch to get bushy plants.

Tetrapanax

Araliaceae

Totally Hardy

The rice paper plant, *Tetrapanax papyrifer* AGM (Z6) is one of the most striking plants available to exotic gardeners. Although originating in Taiwan, it is generally hardy and easy to grow. It will achieve at least 3m (10ft) making a well-branched shrub, clothed with deeply cut, almost ragged, palmate leaves. Cream coloured flowers may be produced in late summer, but these are not attractive. In a mild winter, *Tetrapanax* is semi-evergreen, retaining its foliage until spring. In harsh winters, it will drop its foliage but readily leaf up again the next spring.

As well as the basic species, there is a superior form called 'Rex' that is stronger growing and has bigger leaves. When young they both make excellent container plants, which can then be planted when they get too big. Both are inclined to sucker, sometimes a surprising distance from the main plant. Suckers can be removed as a means of propagation but are not particularly easy to establish. Overwinter young plants under unheated glass.

Thalia

Marantaceae

Generally Hardy

Thalia dealbata, sometimes called the blue water canna, is a useful aquatic to grow as a marginal in shallow water at the side of an exotic pool. The foliage

The exotic looking *Thalia dealbata* is an aquatic plant, needing shallow water at the side of a pool or stream.

is an elongated spade shape, held on long willowy stems, growing to about 90cm (3ft). In late summer it produces spikes of small blue flowers. Reports of hardiness vary. Said to be hardy to Z8 or lower, but to be sure of overwintering, take some under frost-free glass in the autumn and keep moist over winter.

Thunbergia

Acanthaceae

Half Hardy

Although there are many species in this genus, it is mentioned here for the colourful annual climber *Thunbergia alata* (Z10), known as black-eyed Susan. It is a fast growing, twining climber, with heart-shaped leaves and brilliant orange flowers with black centres. It is also available in yellow or white, and without the black centre, which rather seems to miss the point! 'Susie Mixed' has a traditional mix of colours and 'African Sunset' has some great burnished and two-tone tints. They make about 1.5m (5ft) of growth in a season. Grow annually from seed sown in mid spring in a warm greenhouse.

Tibouchina

Melastomataceae

Half hardy

Included for the wonderful blue flowered shrub *Tibouchina urvilleana* (syn *semidecandra*) (Z13). Sadly this one is totally tender and must be returned to the greenhouse for the winter, but it makes a wonderful specimen for a large tub to be brought out for summer display. Overwinter at around 13°C (55°F) and propagate by cuttings.

Tibouchina semidecandra is a tender shrub so best grown in a large tub, enjoyed outside in summer and returned to the greenhouse in winter.

Trachycarpus

Arecaceae/Palmae

Totally Hardy

This genus includes the Chusan palm, one of the few palms that are totally frost hardy in temperate areas. *Trachycarpus fortunei* AGM (Z7) comes from subtropical Asia but is tough and trouble free. It produces typical fans of dark green leaves from a single stem. Old specimens can eventually get to 20m (70ft), but growth is very slow so they are unlikely to be a problem. Mature specimens may produce yellow flowers, followed by attractive blue-black fruit. When young they also grow well in a large pot or tub as patio specimens. Grow in a well-drained fertile soil. Can be propagated from seed but because of its slow growth rate is probably best purchased.

Tradescantia

Commelinaceae

Borderline Hardy

The tradescantias are well known as the windowsill plants, often called wandering Jew. They are easy, fast-growing foliage plants that make a carpet of small pointed leaves with various leaf colourings. *Tradescantia zebrina* AGM (Z9) has prettily marked silver, green and purple leaves, and *T. pallida* AGM (Z9) has rich lustrous purple foliage. It is sold in the trade as 'Purple Sabre'. None exceed 20cm (9in) in height but most are spreading. Often sold as tender, but some gardeners report success with overwintering these outside with a mulch. To be safe, propagate by tip cuttings and overwinter under glass at around 10°C (50°F).

Verbena

Verbenaceae

Generally Hardy and Half hardy

Verbenas are mainly natives of dry areas of tropical and subtropical America, but many have proved amazingly tough and hardy. Most are low growing ground-hugging plants. Try the rich cerise 'Sissinghurst' AGM (Z10) or the paler pink 'Silver Anne' AGM (Z10), which is also deliciously scented. If given a warm spot and good drainage, they may last from year to year and will make sizeable spreading cushions around 25cm × 90cm (9in × 3ft), covered in summer flowers. There are also many modern named cultivars from both seed and cuttings.

OPPOSITE PAGE: **The delicate purple flower is** *Verbena bonariense*, **which can be used in all sorts of situations, allowing it to self-seed and grow as an infill plant.**

V. bonariense AGM (Z8) is a taller type reaching to 90cm (3ft), with willowy stems carrying small heads of purplish pink flowers. It is one of those useful filigree plants which provide height in a planting but are thin enough that they do not block a view – you can see through them. It is grown from seed, and if left alone, will self-seed and appear all over the place but is rarely a nuisance. *V. venosa* (Z8) is very similar, but shorter and more of a pale lilac.

Victoria

Nymphaceae

Half Hardy

This is a genus of tropical water lilies, particularly noted for *Victoria amazonica* (Z10), the largest of all water lilies. Generally only seen in tropical climates or stove houses in botanic gardens, under ideal conditions it will produce gigantic floating circular leaves over 3m (10ft) in diameter. It is said that Joseph Paxton, who first grew it successfully in 1894, took inspiration from the plant's vein structure for his design for the Crystal Palace. Flowers are white the first night they open, changing to pink the second night. Some intrepid exotic gardeners have had varying success with this outside in temperate regions. If you want to try, you will need a warm pool or a heated aquatic planter to grow it. Under temperate conditions, leaves will be much smaller, but it is still an impressive plant in an exotic setting. It is grown annually from seed.

Vitis

Vitaceae

Totally Hardy

This is the family containing fruiting vines, but mentioned here for *Vitis coignetiae* AGM (Z6), a vigorous, exotic-looking deciduous climber, producing huge dinnerplate-sized leaves which turn brilliant orange in autumn before dropping. It climbs by tendrils and will reach 15m (50ft) but can be pruned in winter, like any other grapevine. You may also like to try *V. vinifera* 'Purpurea' AGM (Z6), which has smaller leaves in a deep rich purple. Although it does produce tiny purple grapes, they are barely edible. Both can be propagated by hardwood cuttings outdoors in winter.

Washingtonia

Arecaceae/Palmae

Borderline Hardy

The two fan palms listed here are natives of parts of western USA, such as California and northwest Mexico. It is only recently that temperate gardeners have started dabbling with them, some with amazing success, although it is doubtful that they will ever reach the immense size that are a familiar sight in warmer locations. *Washingtonia filifera* AGM (Z9) eventually makes a very slender trunk with a smallish head of foliage. Its close relative *W. robusta* (Z9) is slower growing and makes a thicker trunk, with a more substantial crown. Both are very much gambles in temperate gardens.

Yucca

Agavaceae

Totally Hardy

Yet another group of 'spikies' and very useful ones, as most species are totally hardy. They come from hot dry areas of central and North America, so are ideal for arid plantings. All have wonderful architectural outlines of lance-shaped leaves from a central rosette and a bonus of white, bell-shaped flowers on spectacular spikes, often shooting up to nearly 2m (6ft). Most are monocarpic, which means

that after flowering, the main shoot will die, although this is usually replaced by sideshoots.

Yucca filamentosa AGM (Z5) is clump-forming, with dark green leaves trimmed with curly white threads, and grows to about 75cm (30in). Another good species is *Y. flaccida* (Z5), also with clumps of green leaves. As the name would suggest, the leaves are less rigid. The cultivar 'Ivory' AGM is probably the best one to grow, for its creamy flowers which are produced in great profusion on a huge spike in late summer, often lasting well into the autumn. *Y. gloriosa* AGM (Z7) makes short branched stems, which with time give the plant a short, stocky tree-like appearance. The rosettes of leaves are attached to the top of each stem. Flowering is again in late summer. There are good vigorous variegated forms of both *Y. filamentosa* and *Y. gloriosa*. In addition 'Bright Edge' AGM and 'Golden Sword' AGM are both excellent cultivars but less vigorous.

For a slightly different effect, try *Yucca rostrata* (Z5), which makes a plant with a distinct trunk and an almost spherical mop of narrow greyish-blue foliage, probably under 1m (4ft) tall. In time, it may become multi-stemmed. *Y. elephantipes* AGM (Z9) is generally thought of as a tender houseplant, but some gardeners have had success with it in sheltered locations, achieving considerable size. All yuccas need a well-drained, hot sunny location.

Zantedeschia

Araceae

Totally Hardy and Half Hardy

Generally known as arum or calla lilies, these are tuberous perennials with lush green foliage and funnel shaped flowers, correctly known as spathes. The plain white *Zantedeschia aethiopica* AGM (Z6) is the most familiar, although there is also 'Green Goddess' AGM which has green spathes splashed with white, and 'Kiwi Blush' which is a very soft pale pink. In full growth will make about 90cm (3ft). All these like a

This spiky plant is *Yucca gloriosa* 'Variegata', grown for its striking foliage as well as its conspicuous flower spikes.

damp soil, such as alongside a pool, but otherwise are undemanding and hardy.

There are also various hybrid arums in amazingly vivid colours, most of which are tender and require frost-free greenhouse conditions to start them off. They are not always easy to bring into growth, and the tubers tend to be expensive. Probably best purchased as flowering plants and used as a little late spot colour.

Zea

Graminae/Poaceae

Half Hardy

And finally we come to a genus that is included, not for the related sweetcorn or cattle feed, which it does include, but for the variegated grass *Zea mays* 'Gracillima' (Z10), which may also come under various other cultivar names. It is in fact the variegated form of maize, growing to just over 1m (4ft), with narrow foliage striped with white or pink. Use it for height and amongst bright coloured foliage or flowers. It is grown annually from seed sown in a warm greenhouse in mid spring.

FURTHER INFORMATION

Exotic Gardens in the UK

The Abbey Garden (Isle of Tresco) Traditional Mediterranean garden in favourable climate, just off the Cornish coast.
www.tresco.co.uk/see/abbey-garden/

Abbotsbury Subtropical Gardens (Dorset) A very old garden but filled with mature exotics and tender plants in a wonderful setting.
www.abbotsbury-tourism.co.uk/gardens.htm

Cotswold Wildlife Park and Gardens (Burford in Oxfordshire) 160 acres of parkland and gardens with many animals and beautiful gardens; hardy and tender exotic plantings everywhere but particularly within the old walled garden.
www.cotswoldwildlifepark.co.uk/

East Ruston Old Vicarage (Norwich) Vast modern garden with many areas, including formal exotic garden, Californian border and desert wash plus Mediterranean garden; exotic species throughout the garden.
www.e-ruston-oldvicaragegardens.co.uk/

Great Dixter (Northiam, East Sussex) Historic garden created by the late Christopher Lloyd including a formal exotic garden planted primarily with tender exotics.
www.greatdixter.co.uk/

Jon Kelf's Jungle Garden (Norwich) Built on a sloping site with five levels of decking surrounded by densely packed, exotic style planting including palms, bamboos, bananas, gingers and ferns.
Contact jonkelf@yahoo.co.uk

Melissa and Keith Scott's Exotic Garden (outside Norwich) With an eclectic mix of plants from bananas, aroids, bamboos and palms that evoke the jungle to cacti, succulents and yuccas more associated with the desert; garden open by appointment to individuals and small groups,
Contact info@melissascott.co.uk

South West Gardens (Devon and Cornwall) Many gardens throughout these counties feature exotic plantings that flourish in this mild climate; look out for Overbecks, Trewidden, Coleton Fishacre, Trebah, Trelissick, Heligan, Glendurgan, Lamorran House, Trengwainton and of course the Eden Project.

University Park (Nottingham) 300 acres of grounds and gardens but in particular the walled garden of Highfields House, filled with bamboos, bananas, palms, hardy and tender exotics, originally planted by the author.
www.nottingham.ac.uk/estate/friends.htm

Will Giles's Exotic Garden (Norwich) A magnificent and inspiring one-acre garden in the centre of the city, incorporating hardy and tender exotics together with arid plantings, plus Victorian summer house, waterfall and tree house.
www.exoticgarden.com/

Exotic Nurseries in the UK

Akamba Easy Exotics (Solihull, near Birmingham) Specialist nursery with exotic plants including arid subjects and garden art.
www.akamba.co.uk/easy_exotics.html

Amulree Exotics (near Norwich)   Hardy and half hardy exotic plants, palms, bananas, cannas and gingers.
www.turn-it-tropical.co.uk/

Architectural Plants (near Chichester)   Specialists in plants that are shapely and exotic.
www.architecturalplants.com/

The Big Plant Company (Ashington, West Sussex) Hardy exotic and architectural plants, 40 miles SW of London. Not all big plants.
www.bigplantnursery.co.uk/

Chiltern Seeds   Smaller seed firm specializing in unusual species with many exotics such as bananas, proteas, eucalyptus and lots more.
www.chilternseeds.co.uk/chilternseeds/index/

Claines Cannas   Extensive list of cannas, including many choice unusual and historic cultivars, some available only in very small quantities.
www.clainescanna.net16.net/

Desert to Jungle   Exotic plants, bamboos, tree ferns, virus free cannas, arid plants and lots more.
www.deserttojungle.com/

Hart Canna   Canna specialist with commercial cultivars, plus many unusual plants in small quantities from the National Collection of Canna.
www.hartcanna.com/

Horn's Garden Centre (Durham) Specialist growers of *Solenostemon* (coleus)
Contact 0191 526 2987.

Jungle Gardens.co.uk   Mail order company with good range of seeds and plants, especially gingers, *Brugmansia* and aroids.
www.jungleseeds.co.uk/

Mulu (near Harrogate) Jungle and arid plants, bamboos, palms, bananas, olives and more.
www.mulu.co.uk/

Palm Centre (Ham, near Richmond, Surrey) Specializes in palms, plus other exotics and arid plants.
www.palmcentre.co.uk/

Read's Nursery (outside Norwich)   Comprehensive list of citrus and tender fruits, plus some exotics such as *Bougainvillea*.
www.readsnursery.co.uk/

Trevena Cross (near Helston in Cornwall)   Many southern hemisphere plants including restios, proteas, succulents, palms, bottlebrushes and tree ferns.
www.trevenacross.co.uk/

Seagrave Nurseries (Barrow Upon Soar, Leicestershire)   Wholesale nursery but open to the public, selling large, specimen imported bamboos, tree ferns, palms and other exotics.
www.seagravenurseries.co.uk/

Urban Jungle (outskirts of Norwich)   Specialist nursery with many hardy and tender exotics; some unusual species.
www.urbanjungle.uk.com/

Other Suppliers and Resources

CED Ltd UK company with many branches supplying huge range of natural stone, paving, rocks, boulders, cobbles and coloured gravels.
www.ced.ltd.uk/

Oasis Exotic Garden Design Run by Paul Spracklin, garden designer with a passion for the exciting effects that can be achieved using sub-tropical style plants. www.oasisdesigns.co.uk/

ScapePlus Garden design and horticultural consultancy business run by Ian Cooke, garden writer and lecturer.
www.scapeplus.com

The Plant Finder On line database, listing thousands of plants and where to obtain them in the UK.
www.rhs.org.uk/rhsplantfinder/

Thermoplanters Heated aquatic planters, distributed by Growth Technology Ltd from a number of sources online and in garden and aquatic centres.
www.growthtechnology.com/gc/thermoplanter.asp

Internet Forums

Growing on the Edge International forum for exotic gardening enthusiasts – discussion, weather, shopping and swapping, photography, photo galleries, plants and gardens
www.growingontheedge.net/index.php

Hardy Tropicals Promotes exotic gardening and the use of exotic plants in general gardening – events, discussion, reference, exotic garden guide.
www.hardytropicals.co.uk/

UK Exotic Gardens Includes plant sales by members, events, information and discussion forum.
www.ukexoticgardens.com/forum/index.php

CoolTropiX Not exactly a forum, but a huge website full of resource material, links and information
www.cooltropix.com/

Read on!

Cooke, Ian, *The Gardener's Guide to Growing Cannas*, David & Charles, 2001.

Cooke, Ian, *The Plantfinder's Guide to Tender Perennials*, David & Charles, 1998.

Giles, Will, *Encyclopaedia of Exotic Plants for Temperate Climates*, Timber Press, 2007.

Giles, Will, *The New Exotic Garden*, Mitchell Beazley, 2000.

Gilmer, Maureen *Palm Springs Style Gardening*, Sunbelt Publications, 2008.

Lloyd, Christopher, *Exotic Planting for Adventurous Gardeners*, Timber Press, 2007.

Schrader, Dennis, *Hot Plants for Cool Climates*, Timber Press, 2005.

INDEX